Girls Getaway Guide
to Key West

Girls Getaway Guide to Key West

Leave Your Baggage at Home

Casey Wohl

ORLANDO, FLORIDA

© 2008 Casey Wohl.

Printed and bound in the United States of America.

All rights reserved. No part of this book may be reproduced or transmitted in any form or by any means, electronic or mechanical, including photocopying, recording, or by an information storage and retrieval system—except by a reviewer who may quote brief passages in a review to be printed in a magazine, newspaper, or on the Web—without permission in writing from the publisher. For information, please contact Gray Dog Publishing, P.O. Box 2589, Orlando, FL 32802, (863) 224-6326.

Every effort has been made to ensure that this book is as up-to-date as possible at press time. Some details, however, such as phone numbers, hours of operation, prices, and travel information are subject to change.

The publisher cannot accept responsibility for any consequences arising from the use of this book, nor third-party websites, and cannot guarantee that any website address featured in this book will be a suitable source of travel information. We value the readers' views and suggestions. Please write to Gray Dog Publishing, P.O. Box 2589, Orlando, FL 32802, wwww.GirlsGetawayGuide.net.

First printing 2008

ISBN 978-0-9790748-4-4

LCCN 2008933987

ATTENTION CORPORATIONS, UNIVERSITIES, COLLEGES, AND PROFESSIONAL ORGANIZATIONS: Quantity discounts are available on bulk purchases of this book for educational, gift purposes, or as premiums for increasing magazine subscriptions or renewals. Special books or book excerpts can also be created to fit specific needs. For information, please contact Gray Dog Publishing, P.O. Box 2589, Orlando, FL 32802, (863) 224-6326.

www.GirlsGetawayGuide.net

CONTENTS

Introduction 7

Chapter 1: **Introduction to Key West** 9
    Key West map • 11
    Duval Street area map • 13

Chapter 2: **Where to Stay** 19

Chapter 3: **Where to Shop** 33

Chapter 4: **Where to Eat** 47

Chapter 5: **Where to Get Pampered** 69

Chapter 6: **Where to Find Galleries, Museums, and
    Nature Attractions** 73

Chapter 7: **Where to Find Nightlife** 95

Chapter 8: **Where to Find Sports, Recreation, and
    Outdoor Activities** 103

Chapter 9: **Where to Go for Side Trips** 115

Chapter 10: **Annual Area Happenings** 119

Chapter 11: **Personal Faves** 127

Chapter 12: **Helpful Sources to Plan Your Trip** 129

Index 135

INTRODUCTION

Key West is one of my favorite destinations for a getaway. I have been visiting this colorful city since I was a child and have watched its transformation from a cheap, touristy town to a vibrant destination filled with art, culture, outdoor activities, water sports, history, beauty, charm, shopping, dining, nightlife, and so much more.

Key West offers a unique combination of fun and sun, land and sea and excitement, day and night. There is so much to do and see. Take a walk through historic Old Town and view hundreds of examples of 19th-century architecture. Sail just seven miles offshore and experience the only living reef in the continental U.S. Tour the homes of Harry Truman and Ernest Hemingway. Enjoy deep sea and flats sports fishing, boating, diving, snorkeling, kayaking, parasailing, sunbathing, and jet skiing. Join the sunset party at Mallory Square pier or take a fabulous sunset cruise. Visit some unique museums and experience Key West's funky vibes and unique heritage in art galleries, shops, boutiques, hotels, and restaurants. According to legend, once Key West sand gets in your shoes, you'll return again and again. With a laid-back atmosphere, abundance of activities, fun-loving lifestyle, and fabulous weather, Key West makes a perfect destination for a girls getaway.

For the latest news and help in planning your girls getaway to Key West, visit www.GirlsGetawayGuide.net.

CHAPTER 1

Introduction to Key West

First recorded by Spanish explorers in 1513, this tiny island (or "key" as it is called because of the Spanish settlement; "*cayo*" means "shoal" or "reef" in Spanish) is just two by four miles. Always attracting freethinkers and fun lovers, Key West has a unique charm and character that have been maintained throughout the years. It is almost 100 miles from Cuba and is located due south of Cleveland, Ohio. Forty-two bridges connect the more than 800 keys that stretch more than 180 miles. The only way to drive to Key West is via U.S. 1, which dead-ends in Key West and is the longest road in the U.S., stretching all the way north to Ft. Kent, Maine.

The name "Conch" (pronounced "conk") is given to anyone native to Key West. If you have lived in Key West for more than seven years, you are a "freshwater conch." In 1982 Key West was designated "The Conch Republic." More than 25,000 people reside on the island, and most of them are on "island time," so leave your schedules behind.

Key West is known for many things. One is the long list of famous U.S. personalities who have made the island a home or destination retreat, including Standard Oil magnate Henry Flagler, fashion designer Calvin Klein, actress Kelly McGillis, naturalist John James Audubon, writer Ernest Hemingway, President Harry S. Truman, playwright Tennessee Williams, poet Robert Frost, Cuban freedom fighter José Marti, and singer Jimmy Buffett.

Key West is known for its chickens. In many parts of town chickens run wild. The abundance of chickens is due to the roosters that were let loose after Cuban cockfighting was outlawed. Today, Key West is a bird sanctuary, and anyone who harms birds will be fined $250.

The island, being only a few square miles, has a small-town atmosphere with a cosmopolitan flair. Diverse from its inception, Key West was established by a mix of English, Bahamian, and Cuban settlers. The island population of approximately 25,000 year-round residents continues to support diversity through its "live-and-let-live" attitude.

> "*Maturity is a phase. Adolescence is forever.*"
>
> —CARTOONIST JULES FEIFFER

Introduction to Key West ♦ 11

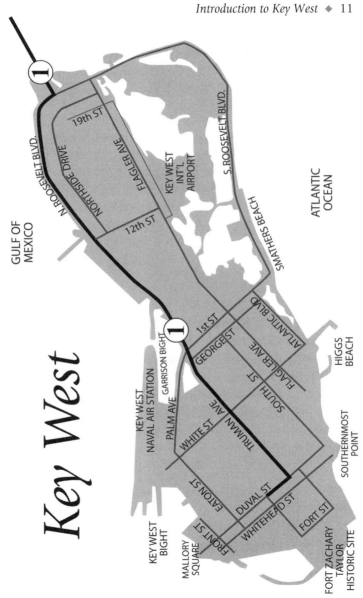

When to Visit

Key West is beautiful and temperate all year round, but there are definitely ideal times to visit. The peak season is from December through April or May. The air temperatures average around 80°F during the day, the water is cool but still comfortable, and there is absolutely no threat of frost, ice, or snow in the "winter" months. During hurricane season, which runs from June through November of every year, the weather tends to be hotter, wetter, and more humid. Keep in mind that the height of hurricane season is August and September. Hotel rates in Key West are typically at their most economical during this time of year.

Getting to Key West

Key West is not as inaccessible as one might think. A lot of people fly into Miami International Airport and either rent a car and drive three hours south to Key West, take the Key West Express Ferry, or hop on a commuter flight into Key West International Airport. The Key West airport doesn't service very many direct flights. Most flights to Key West are routed through Miami, Ft. Lauderdale, Tampa, or Orlando. Another option is to hop on a Greyhound bus from Miami. Greyhound serves Key West to and from Miami. It is around a five-hour ride and costs about $40.

There is also the Key West Express, a ferry service operating from Fort Myers and Marco Island on the western coast of

Introduction to Key West ◆ 13

Old Town Key West

Florida. The ride is approximately five hours long, and the views are spectacular. The ferry also operates from Miami.

If you drive to Key West, it is highly recommended that you watch your speed along U.S. 1 through the Keys. Speed is strictly enforced in order to safeguard the Key deer population.

Getting Around

Driving a car on your own is not recommended in Key West. This is mostly due to the parking headaches. If you do drive to Key West and want to drive around the city on your own, there are parking meters and a municipal parking garage.

You can rent a scooter or bicycle to get around Key West, which is a great way to see the sights, and they are much easier to park than a car. There are rental shops all over Key West. The best way to see Key West (and the cheapest) is simply by walking around on foot.

Miscellaneous Information

- Key West follows Eastern Standard Time (EST).
- Hurricane season is from June through November of each year, with the peak times during August and September.
- Key West is a casual city. Even in the most upscale of restaurants, you can wear comfortable shorts. No ties or jackets are ever required.
- Don't miss the nightly celebration of the sunset in Mallory Square. It's a Key West tradition.

Introduction to Key West ◆ 15

Duval Street

Running from the Gulf of Mexico at the north end to the Atlantic Ocean in the south, Duval Street is the "main drag" of Old Town Key West and the place to do the world-famous Duval Crawl. This "crawl" is the grueling task of strolling the street and stopping in at all the 100 or so bars, pubs, and clubs that line Duval and its neighboring roads. Duval also features many wonderful shops, art galleries, boutiques, restaurants, and cafés. Be sure to wave to your friends back home from the live camera at Duval Street, which is located on the corner of Duval and Green Street under the Sloppy Joe's awning.

Mallory Square

Every evening at sunset, the fun-loving residents of the "Conch Republic" throw a party in this large seaside square, complete with entertainers of all sorts. Located on the northern side of Duval Street, the square overlooks the Gulf of Mexico and is a popular destination for visitors. There is no admission to join the sunset party, but I advise you to arrive early. Once the sun is safely tucked away and the jugglers, mimes, musicians and street artists disperse, the city moves to a different beat. A night beat. The vibrant streets, filled with sidewalk cafés, open-air bars, legendary pubs, and world-class restaurants, come alive.

> *"If you obey all the rules, you miss all the fun."*
> —KATHERINE HEPBURN

16 ◆ *Girls Getaway Guide to Key West*

Bahama Village

An archway across Petronia Street at Duval lets you know you are entering this 16-block, largely African-American neighborhood, which offers a tiny slice of island culture. At the entrance is the Bahama Market, featuring handicrafts and an open-air flea market; farther along is Blue Heaven. This area is southwest of downtown in the Old Town area. New restaurants and stores are popping up in the historic Bahama Village neighborhood, which was settled in the nineteenth century by Bahamian immigrants. Hemingway loved coming here to mix with the hard-working locals at boxing matches and arm-wrestling contests.

Old Town

Old Town is the name given to the historic district of the island, which is basically the western half of the island. Here you'll find several tourist attractions. In 1983 the area was expanded to 5,400 acres and 2,485 historic buildings, bounded by Emma, Whitehead, White, and South Streets, Mallory Square, and the Atlantic Ocean.

Historic Seaport

The island's seafaring tradition lives on at the renovated Historic Seaport district, known locally as the Key West Bight. Dozens of shrimp boats once called this harbor home.

These days, "the Bight" is a popular place to arrange a day on the water, whether you are a diver, snorkeler, fisherman, or ecotourist. Others come just to stroll along the harbor walk or dine at one of the many restaurants.

Beaches (for more details see Chapter 8)

South Beach is located at the end of Duval Street. It is a shallow, sandy beach typically packed with tourists.

Smathers Beach, located on Roosevelt Blvd., is Key West's largest public beach, running along the southern shore of the island for almost two miles. Beach activities range from tanning to volleyball and watersport/beachsport rentals. Admission is free. Vendors offer snacks, beverages, chairs, and rafts.

Ft. Zachary Taylor Beach is located in Ft. Zachary Taylor State Park, which requires an admission fee. It is the locals' favorite beach and is very popular for snorkeling, with lots of tropical fish. Be careful as it gets deep quickly and has a rocky bottom, so it's recommended you wear water shoes.

Higgs Beach is free to everyone and located on the eastern side of the island.

Resort Beaches—As far as resorts, the Casa Marina, Reach Resort, Hyatt Beach House Resort (Hyatt Vacation Club), and Pier House all have good beaches.

CHAPTER 2

Where to Stay

There are numerous accommodation choices in Key West, from high-end resorts to charming bed & breakfasts to thrifty picks; the selection is varied. You have to remember that Key West is an island and often the accommodations were converted from old buildings, so be sure to ask lots of questions regarding your choice, such as if the location offers parking, amenities, private baths, and so on. Key West lodging costs are often determined by the time of year, holidays, and special events. Most businesses typically follow a high season (January through May), mid-season (June through mid-August and October through mid-December), and a low season (mid/late August through September); however, some will vary. Lodging rates in this chapter are represented by a range that reflects the least expensive to the most expensive. To determine exact rates for your trip, please contact the business directly. Other alternatives not listed include houses and condos for rent.

Avalon Bed & Breakfast

1317 Duval St.; (305) 294-8233
www.avalonbnb.com

This restored Victorian home is just a few steps away from the Southernmost Point and across from the Key West Butterfly & Nature Conservatory. Room options include: queen rooms, king rooms, double queen rooms, small queen rooms, and the king poolside cottage. Rates range from $89–$289 and include a continental breakfast buffet daily on the front porch.

Banyan Resort

323 Whitehead St.; (305) 296-7786
www.thebanyanresort.com

Conveniently located two blocks from Mallory Square and three blocks from Ft. Zachary Taylor State Park and Beach, the Banyan Resort originally consisted of six homes that were constructed as private residences during the mid-1800s. The individual owners of these properties decided to combine their interests in the early 1980s and convert them into "The Banyan Guest House." In August 2007 Banyan was designated a Green Lodging Facility. The unbelievable banyan tree in back of the property was planted in 1872. This resort is a popular place for celebs, such as Calvin Klein, to stay. Today, the Banyan Resort is predominantly a timeshare, but it does rent rooms as well. Property amenities include: two solar-heated swimming pools, a whirlpool, free wireless Internet, full concierge services, guest laundry facilities, bicycle and scooter rentals, poolside Tiki bar, gas grills located under the banyan tree, and on-site parking. Each suite (studio, one or two bedroom) in this tropical, historic resort features the comforts of home, including a full kitchen, ceiling fans, air conditioning, cable TV, verandahs, a coffee maker, a microwave, and everything you need. Hotel rates range from $200–$410.

Budget Key West

1031 Eaton St.; (305) 294-3333
www.historickeywestinns.com

This 17-room hotel located in the historic district is a great thrifty pick. You cannot miss the older, yellow house that is two blocks from the Key West harbor and a short walk to Duval Street. Rooms are clean and simple and offer 1–2 queen beds and private baths, as well as ceiling fans, refrigerators, TV, and A/C. There is no pool, but chaise lounge chairs provide a nice sunning area. The hotel is AAA approved with two diamonds and is a very nice value in a small, historic hotel. Rates range from $89–$299.

Casa Marina Resort & Beach Club

1500 Reynolds St.; (305) 296-3535
www.casamarinaresort.com

The Casa Marina is one of the oldest hotels on the island and is listed on the National Register of Historic Places. Construction began in 1912 and was finally completed in 1921. The resort recently underwent a full five-star, $43 million renovation, so the property features modern-day amenities. It has the largest private beach in Key West at 1,100 feet. While residing in one of the resort's 311 guest rooms and suites, you can indulge in

22 ◆ Girls Getaway Guide to Key West

beachside massages, a private pier, relaxing hammocks, two oceanfront swimming pools, private cabanas, scooter and bike rentals, water equipment rentals located directly on the beach, onsite dining, and private balconies for panoramic ocean and beach views. Overnight parking is available for $10 per day; valet parking is $20 per day. Rates range from $169–$679.

Casa 325

325 Duval St.; (305) 292-0011
www.casa325.com

Located on Duval Street in a restored Conch Victorian building, Casa 325 provides studios and 1–2 bedroom suites that feature hardwood floors, handcrafted queen-sized beds and kitchenettes, each uniquely decorated with a tropical island theme. All rooms are non-smoking and have color TVs, ceiling fans, A/C, microwaves, refrigerators, coffeemakers, and toasters. A pool is located on-site; limited on-site parking is available for $10/night. Rates range from $115–$475.

Crowne Plaza Key West—La Concha

430 Duval St.; (305) 296-2991
www.laconchakeywest.com

When you stay at the Crowne Plaza Key West—La Concha, you will feel all the history that surrounds this beautiful hotel, which is located on Duval near Whitehead Street. Carl E. Aubuchon built this seven-story Key West landmark, which first opened in January 1926, to provide the city with a "first-class hotel." The newest hotel (at that time) on the island had marble floors, private baths, elevators, and other luxuries new to Key West accommodations. It was no surprise that the hotel was an immediate success with wealthy tourists and dignitaries. The 1929 stock market crash and hurricanes caused a severe drop in tourism in subsequent years. Then, newer hotels were built in Key West, which stole the spotlight from the La Concha. Through it all, the La Concha survived and played host to its share of famous personalities, such as Ernest Hemingway and Tennessee Williams. Today, the hotel features newly-renovated guest rooms, including one-bedroom suites that combine the hotel's original 1920s style with modern-day comfort. The second-floor guestrooms offer walkout balconies overlooking Duval Street, which are perfect for people watching. Wireless high-speed Internet and a Starbucks are located in the lobby. The seventh floor of the hotel features a bar with an outdoor balcony; it is one of the most popular spots in all of Key West. It is best known for the fabulous views of Key West's sunsets and bird's-eye view of the island. The hotel restaurant, Jack's Seafood Shack, offers breakfast, lunch, dinner, and great drinks. Hotel rates range from $159–$849.

DoubleTree Grand Key Resort

3990 South Roosevelt Blvd.; (305) 293-1818
www.grandkeyresort.com

Located near the airport and away from the action on Duval Street, the 216-room DoubleTree is the ideal location for those who want to be near the Key West scene but also able to escape it during their stay.

Grand Key Resort provides complimentary shuttle service to Key West International Airport, Grand Key Resort Beach Club,

Historic Old Town, Key West Golf Course, and most marinas. The zero-barrier entry pool is nestled in a nice natural island setting surrounded by native flora and a waterfall complete with a poolside restaurant and available cabana massages. Dining options include the elegant Palm Haven, the casual Sanctuary Lounge, the poolside Gumbo Limbo Bar, or Room Service. Parking is available for $10/day. Hotel rates range from $169–$500.

Duval Gardens Bed & Breakfast

1012 Duval St.; (305) 292-3379
www.duvalgardens.com

Located on the quiet end of Duval, this small B&B provides queen and king rooms as well as queen kitchenettes. A small, heated pool is available for guests, and a continental breakfast is provided on the front porch each morning. Amenities include full private baths, A/C, mini-refrigerator, hair dryer, color cable TV, and complimentary continental breakfast. Irons and coffee makers are available by request. Limited off-street parking is available. Rates range from $89–$229.

Gardens Hotel

526 Angela St.; (305) 294-2661
www.gardenshotel.com

Owner Kate Miano has done an amazing job of transforming this property into a luxurious oasis of tropical gardens and classic elegance. This hotel has received several awards, including *Condé Nast Traveler's* Gold List of Best Places to Stay, *New York Times'* The List, Zagat's Best in Key West, and TripAdvisor's Best

Where to Stay ◆ 25

Hidden Gem. The 17 rooms and suites feature HD flat-screen TVs, refrigerators, coffee makers, designer linens, A/C, ceiling fans, spa robes, Internet access, and free calls. The pool bar is the perfect hangout, and a complimentary island breakfast is served each day. The Helio Gardens Gallery is housed on-site as well. Rates range from $200–$435 for the low season, $265–$525 mid-season, $325–$645 high season, and $385–$705 for special events.

Island City House Hotel

411 William St.; (305) 294-5702
www.islandcityhouse.com

Located in the heart of Old Town and made up of three houses (Island City House, The Cigar House, and The Arch House) that share common areas, this property also offers complimentary island breakfast buffet each morning in the shaded brick court-yard. Studios and one- and two-bedroom units are available. The Island City House is a three-story Victorian mansion built in the late 1880s. This house offers 12 parlor suites decorated in complete Victorian décor, including antiques and white lace curtains. The Cigar House is a three-story structure made of red cypress wood that recreates the Alfonso Cigar factory, which occupied the site 100 years ago. This house offers six parlor suites decorated in a tropical plantation style. The Arch House was originally a Victorian carriage house built in the late 1800s and is the only standing carriage house on the island. It offers six suites furnished in a casual island style. Amenities include a pool, A/C, gardens, and television, and some units have a private porch or deck. Prices range from $150–$420.

Key West Bed & Breakfast, The Popular House

415 William St.; (305) 296-7274
www.keywestbedandbreakfast.com

Located in the William Russell house (circa 1898) and listed in the National Register of Historic Places, this three-story Victorian home is located in the heart of Key West's "Old Town." The building is alive with bright colors and cozy furnishings, providing the perfect escape for visitors. Each of the eight guest rooms is decorated with a vivid Caribbean flair featuring hardwood floors, exposed Dade County pine walls, and high ceilings. Amenities include complimentary breakfast, Jacuzzi, sauna, Bahama fans, and A/C (no pool). The House is filled with personality, great artwork, and flashy color; nonetheless, the prices here are reasonable. Prices range from $59–$175 off-season and $99–$285 in-season.

La Mer Hotel and Dewey House

504/506 South St.; (305) 296-6577
www.LaMerHotel.com

Located next to each other, these two restored Victorian-style properties are on the beach and just steps away from Duval Street. Each of these intimate boutique hotels has a unique, turn-of-the-century feel, spacious rooms, and are connected by lush tropical gardens, towering palms, and brightly colored flowers. Their sense of class and historic charm make them unique among accommodations on the island.

The Victorian-style La Mer Hotel has 11 elegant rooms while the quaint and historic Dewey House has eight. Each offers the kind of luxury accommodations you'd expect from a boutique hotel in Key West—granite wet bars, private balconies or patios, monogrammed robes, British Colonial furnishings, and Jacuzzi tubs. The décor combines a tropical, breezy feel with historic stateliness. Dining options include the Southernmost Beach Café and the Ambrosia Restaurant. Guests enjoy full-service concierge, complimentary parking, wireless Internet access, direct beach access, library, 24-hour front desk, amenities basket, mini-refrigerator, laundry/dry cleaning, daily newspaper, afternoon tea (3:30–5:30 P.M.), and deluxe continental breakfast (8:30–10:30 A.M.) on the Dewey Terrace. Hotel rates range from $169–$449.

Ocean Key Resort & Spa

Zero Duval St.; (305) 296-7701
www.oceankey.com

Ocean Key offers 100 guest rooms and suites decorated in a Key West décor. It's a AAA four-diamond property. Each room has a balcony and Jacuzzi tubs, and the resort's Sunset Pier is the ideal place to watch the sunset and the nightly sunset celebration. The resort features the indulgence of SpaTerre and dining at the delectable Hot Tin Roof, a four-diamond restaurant. The pool overlooks the ocean and is the ideal place to relax with a fabulous view. Rates for standard rooms range from $369–$459; oceanfront rooms range from $509–$699, and the two-bedroom penthouse rents for $2,510–$2,800.

Pier House Resort & Caribbean Spa

One Duval St.; (305) 296-4600
www.pierhouse.com

Providing a casual Key West atmosphere at the end of Duval Street, the Pier House offers a small, private beach with a nice outdoor bar area. The pool area is adequate, and the rooms are basic and clean. If you want the resort feel without the huge resort price, the Pier House is for you. Dining options include the Harbour View Café, Wine Gallery Piano Bar, Chart Room Bar, and the Beach Bar & Grille. Standard room prices are $244/night; ocean view rooms start at $324/night.

Reach Resort

1435 Simonton St.; (305) 296-5000
www.thereachresort.com

Featuring the island's only natural beach in its backyard, the Reach Resort recently underwent full five-star renovations. The resort houses 150 guest rooms, including 76 suites, on five floors, all with private balconies. It offers high-speed Internet access in all guest rooms and suites, a heated outdoor swimming pool, The Sun-Sun Beach Bar & Grill, serving snacks and tropical drinks, a massage studio and health spa with indoor and outdoor body treatments, equipment rental (jet skis, sailboats, kayaks, paddleboats, ocean bikes, and snorkel gear), valet parking, room service, and same-day dry cleaning. Dining options also include the Strip House (dine-in restaurant, in-room, poolside, cocktail, or catered) and Australian Homemade Ice Cream. Rates range from $199–$449.

Simonton Court Historic Inn & Cottages

320 Simonton St.; (800) 944-2687
www.simontoncourt.com

Located in the heart of Old Town and close to Duval Street, Simonton Court displays its charm from the minute you step on the property. The brick walkway meanders through lush flowers and palms that provide a tropical atmosphere. This adult-only B&B offers several accommodation options, including the two-story Inn (which was once a cigar factory), Manor House, six cottages, The Mansion, and townhouse suites. No two options are alike, so it is best to call for details. Each unit has a private bath, A/C, ceiling fans, cable TV, VCR, phones, safe, and refrigerator. The property boasts four pools, and many units offer private porches, sundecks, or Jacuzzis. Continental breakfast is served poolside each morning. Be sure also to inquire about the cancellation policy. Rates: low season $155–$395; high season $245–$515.

Southernmost Hotel on Duval Street

1319 Duval St.; (305) 296-6577
www.southernmostresorts.com

A great location for moderately-priced accommodations, the 127-room Southernmost Hotel on Duval Street also offers two pools with Tiki bars, a Jacuzzi, complimentary parking, no hidden resort fees, and beach and private pier access. Rates range from $99–$265.

You may also inquire about the sister property, Southernmost on the Beach, located at 508 South Street and available at the same phone number. Rates for this property are $169–$369.

Sunset Key Guest Cottages

245 Front St.; (305) 292-5300
www.westin.com/sunsetkey

Girls looking for a secluded and luxurious getaway should consider the 27-acre island of Sunset Key. This island is just 500 yards away from Old Town Key West and is accessible only by a 24-hour daily launch service from The Westin Key West Resort & Marina. Nestled on this tropical oasis are one-, two-, and three-bedroom cottages, each designed in traditional Key West architecture with garden or ocean views. The cottages are quaint and charming, complete with pastel wood trimming, wraparound porches with Adirondack chairs, and authentic Victorian-style tin roofs. Each cottage features a living room, dining room, and equipped kitchen that comes pre-stocked with selected food and beverages. Bedrooms boast the Westin's "Heavenly Bed." Lounge on the private white-sand beach in a chaise lounge or under a cabana while beach attendants cater to your group's needs. Other amenities include a free-form swimming pool, two whirlpools, Flippers Pool Bar, and Latitudes Beach Café. You can also have the chef prepare your favorite meal in your cottage or order from the in-room dining menu. Rates range from $495–$2,225.

The Westin Key West Resort & Marina

245 Front St.; (305) 294-4000
www.Westin.com/keywest

A waterfront resort with 178 guest rooms and deluxe suites, the Westin offers great service and amenities, which include a full-service marina complete with all types of water sports options, a courtyard heated pool and Jacuzzi, fitness room with massage therapy and spa treatments, Bistro 245 (a waterfront restaurant), and poolside bar and dining. Guests can enjoy the Sunset Deck with live music and tropical drinks, access to a secluded beach area, and nearby shopping along Harborwalk and on Duval. This is a great property, but we did notice a crowd of people and blockage of the view when the cruise ships dock, so be sure to ask about the cruise ship schedule during your stay. Dogs under 40 pounds are welcome. Prices range from $229–$829.

> *"The better part of one's life consists of friendships."*
> —ABRAHAM LINCOLN

CHAPTER 3

Where to Shop

Without a "mall" on the island, Key West shopping is focused around shops and boutiques unique to the area. Although you will find brand-name stores such as Banana Republic, Express, and Coach, this chapter focuses on the shopping you cannot find at home. Key West hosts some great shopping, such as art, island apparel, jewelry, home and garden, culinary, books, and, of course, key lime pie.

> "Some women hold up dresses that are so ugly and they always say the same thing: 'This looks much better on.' On what? Fire?"
>
> —RITA RUDNER

34 ◆ *Girls Getaway Guide to Key West*

7 Artists Gallery

604 Duval St.; (305) 293-0411
www.7artistskeywest.com

A great place to find unique gifts and fine art from Key West, this gallery provides a variety of original wearable artwork in precious and semi-precious stones with 14K gold and sterling silver. Open daily 10:00 A.M.–10:00 P.M.

Abaco Gold

418 Front St.; (305) 296-0086

Just off Duval, this store offers bejeweled sandals and a wide variety of jewelry, nautical themed accessories, and more. Open Monday to Saturday 9:00 A.M.–9:00 P.M.; Sunday 11:00 A.M.–6:00 P.M.

American Apparel

608 Duval St.; (305) 292-0200
www.americanapparel.net

Hot in Key West and want to show some skin? This somewhat promiscuous chain of clothing stores is appropriately situated on Duval Street and offers some suggestive marketing campaigns. In addition, conscious consumers will feel good knowing these wares were manufactured in non-sweatshop conditions in the U.S. Open Monday to Saturday 10:00 A.M.–10:00 P.M.; Sunday noon–8:00 P.M.

The Beach House Swimwear

714 Duval St.; (800) 371-7763
www.thebeachhouseswimwear.com

Although small, this store features more than 4,000 designer and brand-name swimsuits, such as Juicy Couture, Calvin Klein, and Gottex, as well as sarongs and cover-ups. Open daily 10:00 A.M.–9:00 P.M.

Beads of Distinction

218 Whitehead St. #4; (305) 293-8840
www.beadsofdistinction.com

Key West's only bead shop has a vast array of jewelry fashioned from metal, glass, seed, and bone beads originating from all over the world, including Africa and Bali. Here you can also take a beading class and find beading tools and instruction books. Open Monday to Thursday 10:00 A.M.–6:00 P.M.; Friday and Saturday 10:00 A.M.–7:00 P.M.; Sunday noon–6:00 P.M.

Besame Mucho

315 Petronia St.; (305) 294-1928
www.besamemucho.net

A unique shop that features a variety of goods ranging from Mexican jewelry, artwork, and Kiehl's products. Its shabby chic vibe provides a cozy shopping experience while you browse home goods, souvenirs, and much more. A must visit! Open Monday to Saturday 10:00 A.M.–6:00 P.M.; Sunday 10:00 A.M.–4:00 P.M.

Biton

404 Duval St.; (305) 296-4617

Catering to clients who live in comfortable clothes, such as linens, Biton spans three spaces on Duval. One store caters to women and the other to men, with the main store catering to the Martha's Vineyard beachcomber look. Open daily 9:00 A.M.– midnight.

Blue

718 Caroline St.; (305) 292-5172
www.blueislandstore.com

A unique shop that combines island attitude with urban trends. Owner/jewelry designer David Symons provides a wonderful jewelry collection to peruse.

The Blue Cat

291 Front St. #6; (305) 293-9339

For pet owners, no visit to Key West is complete without a stop at The Blue Cat. This boutique has designer collars, bowls, doormats, shirts, hats, toys, and totes to make your favorite pet look fabulous. Open daily 10:00 A.M.–5:30 P.M.

Cocktail Party

808 Duval St.; (305) 295-9100

A must-stop for fun-loving girls, be sure to shop here for essential bar amenities, including cocktail shakers, fun napkins, martini glasses, and more. Open daily 10:00 A.M.–6:00 P.M.

Where to Shop ◆ 37

Commotion

800 Caroline St.; (305) 292-3364

A quaint boutique full of casual, linen, and linen-esque clothing (including flax) for shoppers looking for the ultimate in relaxing clothing and accessories. Open daily 9:30 A.M.–6:00 P.M.

Congress Jewelers

128 Duval St.; (305) 296-5885
www.congressjewelers.com

This store features a nice selection of nautical and sea-themed jewelry created by Congress's own designers. They are also an authorized dealer of Rolex, Breitling, Tag Heuer, and more. Open Monday to Saturday 10:00 A.M.–9:30 P.M.; Sundays noon–8:30 P.M.

Cuba! Cuba!

814 Duval St.; (305) 295-9442
www.cubacubastore.com

Want to experience Havana shopping? Look no further than Key West's own Cuban shopping experience, featuring arts, crafts, cigar label art, coffee, cigars, books, food, and all you could imagine from Cuba. Open Sunday to Friday 10:00 A.M.–6:00 P.M.; Saturday 10:00 A.M.–10:00 P.M.

Dreaming Goddess Boutique

Your hotel room; (305) 923-9589
www.thedreaminggoddess.com

Big Pine Key fashion designer and silk artist Jasmine Sky will come to where you are staying and provide a free 30-minute consultation to discuss your most flattering colors and styles. She brings her own line of hand-painted resort wear that ranges from shorts and T-shirts to formal wear.

Ego

607 Duval St.; (305) 296-1133

Loud music and loud clothes are found here in this appropriately named store, which is visited frequently by Key West's spring-breaker types. Here you can find T-shirts, Board shorts, and other clothing by designers such as Billabong and Roxy. Open daily 10:00 A.M.–10:00 P.M.

Emeralds International, Inc.

104 Duval St.; (305) 294-2060
www.emeraldsinternational.com

As the name suggests, you can find some amazing green dazzlers at this place. In addition, jewelry made from conch pearls makes a nice showing. Be sure to browse the store for platinum and 18k and 14k gold pieces. You may just find something you cannot live without. Open Monday to Saturday 10:00 A.M.–6:00 P.M.; Sunday 11:00 A.M.–5:00 P.M.

Evan & Elle

725 Duval St.; (305) 295-3530

During my stays in Key West, I always stop by Evan & Elle. This store carries a selection of trendy men's and women's clothing, such as BCBG, True Religion, and Juicy Couture. It's not the place to go for unique take-home gifts, but I always like to browse. Open daily from 9:00 A.M.–midnight.

Fast Buck Freddie's

500 Duval St.; (305) 294-2007
www.fastbuckfreddies.com

Located centrally on Duval, this store is always a stop on my visits to Key West. It was founded in 1979 and is the closest thing to a department store you'll find in Key West. It features great home décor, as well as men's, women's, and children's Keys attire. For laughs, be sure to visit the "adult" room in the back of the store. I usually find fun things to pick up for my girlfriends. Open Monday to Wednesday 10:00 A.M.–6:00 P.M.; Thursday to Friday 10:00 A.M.–8:00 P.M.; Saturday 10:00 A.M.–10:00 P.M.; Sunday 11:00 A.M.–6:00 P.M.

Fresh Produce

400A Duval St.; (305) 293-1970
www.freshproducesportswear.com

Fresh Produce first sprouted in 1984 in Long Beach, California, selling silk-screened T-shirts in bright graphics and custom jewelry at the '84 summer Olympics in the parking lot across from the coliseum. Over the years the concept has remained the same—to bring the emotions, the colors, the sensations, and the leisure of beach life to everyday life through fashion. It was, and is, the life of Thom and Mary Ellen Vernon, the dynamic husband and wife team who started the company and whose vision continues to inspire the Fresh Produce culture. Open Monday to Friday 10:00 A.M.–9:00 P.M.; Saturday 10:00 A.M.–10:00 P.M.; Sunday 11:00 A.M.–8:00 P.M.

Kermit's Key West Key Lime Shoppe

200A Elizabeth St.; (305) 296-0806
www.keylimeshop.com

For girls wanting to taste test all Key West's key lime pies, be sure to visit Kermit's, where you can learn all about key limes, key lime pies, key lime recipes, and key lime gifts. Kermit's offers candy, BBQ sauces, dressings, salsas, cookies, key lime juice, gifts, and much more! Open daily 9:00 A.M.–9:00 P.M.

Key Accents Home & Garden

804 Caroline St.; (305) 293-8555
www.keyaccents.net

Find your entire home and garden needs met here with a Key West flare. This store offers mirrors, accents, furniture, lighting, and fabrics all with expert interior design services. Open Monday to Saturday 10:00 A.M.–5:30 P.M.; Sunday 10:00 A.M.–5:00 P.M.

Key West Aloe

540 Greene St.; (305) 293-1885
www.keywestaloe.com

Aloe has always been used to soothe sunburns, so it is no surprise that the Conch Republic has its own aloe. From Soothing Cucumber Undereye Gel to Key Lime Foot Scrub to Frangipani Body Lotion, this store has something for everyone, including women, men, kids, and pets. Hours: Monday to Saturday 9:00 A.M.–8:00 P.M.; Sunday 10:00 A.M.–6:00 P.M.

Key West Island Books

513 Fleming St.; (305) 294-2904

Carrying new, used, and rare titles, this general bookstore is popular with the Key West literary community. The store specializes in Hemingway, Tennessee Williams, and Florida and Key West writers. Hours: 10 A.M.–9 P.M. daily.

Kino Sandals

107 Fitzpatrick St.; (305) 294-5044
www.kinosandalfactory.com

Those who have purchased Kino sandals usually come back to Key West for another pair. I have girlfriends who have these sandals in every color and others who take orders for their entire family when they plan to visit Key West. These sandals are inexpensive yet very durable and last for years. Started by a Cuban immigrant, Kino Sandals is still a family business and a staple in Key West. Open Monday to Friday 8:30 A.M.–5:30 P.M.; Saturday 9:00 A.M.–5:30 P.M.; Sundays–seasonal.

Lilly Pulitzer

600 Front St.; (305) 295-0995
www.lillypulitzer.com

Don't miss this Palm Beach-inspired resort wear that always features colorful, quality dresses, tops, and pants for women, as well as men's and children's wear. Open Monday to Saturday 9:00 A.M.–8:00 P.M.; Sunday noon–5:00 P.M.

Local Color

276 Margaret St.; (305) 296-5644
www.localcolorkeywest.com

The name is very appropriate as this store offers clothing, jewelry, accessories, and much more, all with "local color." The jewelry is amazing and comes from all over the world. The pink conch is very popular and gorgeous. Open daily 9:00 A.M.–10:00 P.M.

Where to Shop ◆ 43

Peppers of Key West

602 Greene St.; (305) 295-9333
www.peppersofkeywest.com

Known as "the hottest spot on the island," this store is so much fun to visit, and owner Peter will make sure you have a "hot" time. Samples are provided, but you must bring your own beer (as well as some for the staff). Open daily 10:00 A.M.–6:00 P.M.

The Restaurant Store

1111 Eaton St.; (305) 294-7994
www.keywestchef.com

Open to the public, this store carries all the great kitchen items used in restaurants, including top-of-the-line knives, lovely cookware, coffee frothers, pizza oven paddles, specialty food items, and much more. Open Monday to Saturday 9:00 A.M.–6:00 P.M.; Sundays 11:00 A.M.–4:00 P.M.

Shades of Key West

335 Duval St.; (305) 294-0519
302 Front St.; (305) 294-0329

Sunglasses are a must for anyone in Key West, and Shades is just the place to outfit yourself in Gucci, Guess, Maui Jim, Costa Del Mar, or Oakley. In business since 1978, this place has seen sunglass trends come and go but will keep you in style during your visit. Open daily 9:00 A.M.–10:00 P.M. on Duval Street; 9:00 A.M.–8:00 P.M. on Front Street.

Sponge Market

Mallory Square; (305) 294-2555

Stop by the Sponge Market for a virtual overview by fifth-generation Key West native C.B. McHugh, who was born in Key West in 1923. You will learn the process of gathering the sponges and preparing them for market, as well as the different types of sponges. Browse through the merchandise and select your favorite type of sponge. Open daily from 10:00 A.M.–9:00 P.M.

Sugar Apple

917 Simonton St.; (305) 292-0043
www.sugarapplekeywest.com

After too much key lime pie and fried foods, you will be ready for a dose of healthy eating. Sugar Apple provides a plethora of vitamins, granola, homeopathic medicine, and ginseng. Open Monday to Saturday 10:00 A.M.–6:00 P.M.

Sunset Cigar Co.

306 Front St.; (305) 295-0600
www.sunsetcigarco.com

Located in the old Key West Cigar Factory, this historic cigar shop features hundreds of cigars, humidors, and even a cigar lounge. A great place to buy souvenirs for that special guy. Open daily 9:00 A.M.–9:30 P.M.

Truval Village Market Place

1007 Duval St.; (305) 295-9221

From linen, cover-ups, dresses, swimsuits, T-shirts, sandals, towels, and much more, this store has all you need in casual apparel during your time in Key West. Open daily 9:00 A.M.–11:00 P.M.

Voltaire Books Key West

330 Simonton St.; (305) 296-3226
www.voltairebooks.com

A fun, independent bookstore filled with anything and everything you'd want to read during your stay in Key West (and after). Voltaire features a complete list of Key West icons, such as Ernest Hemingway and Tennessee Williams, as well as fiction and nonfiction, local authors, coffee table books, and fun gifts. Owner Christopher Kush and his staff are very helpful and will make you feel at home here. Open daily 10ish–7ish.

CHAPTER 4

Where to Eat

Key West has a vast array of restaurants with almost too many options. Most establishments are casual and offer alcoholic beverages (sometimes during all hours of the day). The seafood is incredible here as there is a robust seafood industry. The island is world-renowned for its cultural diversity, which is evident in the wide selection of restaurants that may be found in the nation's southernmost city.

> *"I never worry about diets. The only carrots that interest me are the number you get in a diamond."*
>
> —MAE WEST

Attire: C=Casual; D=Dressy

Price—Dinner For Two: $=Less than $40;
$$=$40–$60;
$$$=$60–$80;
$$$$=More than $80

Reservations: R=Required; S=Suggested; NR=Not Required

A&B Lobster House

700 Front St. (upstairs); (305) 294-5880
www.aandblobsterhouse.com

Seafood; D/C; $$$; R; Lunch, dinner

Since 1947, the A&B has been a local favorite for fine dining. In fact, when I asked several locals for a nice seafood dining recommendation, they all suggested we eat at A&B. After a nice bottle of wine and a fabulous meal, we are well on our way to enjoying the rest of our evening. Here you will find white tablecloths, fine wine, and wonderful service.

Alonzo's Oyster Bar

700 Front St.; (305) 294-5880
www.alonzosoysterbar.com

Seafood; C; $$; NR; Lunch, dinner

Located underneath A&B, Alonzo's offers a more casual, harbor-side option for those who want to feast on a variety of oysters and other seafood. Situated on the Key West Bight, Alonzo's offers salads, chowders, cocktails, beer, and wine. Open daily 11:00 A.M.–11:00 P.M.

Angelina's Pizza

208 Duval St.; (305) 296-3600
www.angelinaspizzakeywest.com

Italian; C; $; NR; Lunch, dinner, late night

Conveniently located in the middle of several infamous Key West bars, Angelina's is a great stop for a midnight snack. These delicious pies are a great substance to keep you going during those

Where to Eat ◆ 49

long Duval Street nights. Open Monday to Thursday 11:00 A.M.–2:00 A.M.; Friday to Saturday 11:00 A.M.–3:00 A.M.; closed Sunday.

Bad Ass Coffee Company

101 Duval St.; (305) 294-9004
www.badasscoffee.com

Not only do we like the name, we also like this coffee. Wake up with attitude! Bad Ass also offers fruit smoothies, teas, mochas, and lattes, and these can be blended on request. Open daily 8:00 A.M.–9:00 P.M.

Bagatelle Restaurant

115 Duval St.; (305) 296-6609
www.bagatelle-keywest.com

American/Seafood; C; $$; NR; Lunch, dinner

A great place to people watch on Duval, this old Victorian mansion with a wrap-around porch provides great southern charm. Its claim to fame is wonderful seafood, especially the tuna sashimi. The inside bar provides an old "speak easy" feel. A girlfriend reported, "They have all kinds of drinks and cute bartenders." Located one block from Mallory Square.

Banana Café

1211 Duval St.; (305) 294-7227

French; C; $; NR; Breakfast, lunch, dinner

If you love crepes or French food, be sure to visit this quaint café with a French flair. Open daily 8:00 A.M.–3:00 P.M. and 6:00 P.M.–10:00 P.M.

50 ◆ *Girls Getaway Guide to Key West*

Blond Giraffe

802 Duval St.; (305) 293-7874
614 Front St.; (305) 296-2020
107 Simonton St.; (305) 293-6667
1209 Truman Ave.; (305) 295-6776
412 Greene St.; (305) 293-7874
www.blondgiraffe.com

Key West's answer to Starbucks (as in one on every corner), the Blond Giraffe's key lime pies were voted "Best Key Lime Pie in Key West" at the 1999 Key Lime Pie Festival. You can even see the pies being made at the Simonton Street store.

Blue Heaven

729 Thomas St.; (305) 296-8666
http://Blueheavenkw.homestead.com

Island fare; C; $$; NR; Breakfast, lunch, dinner

A must-stop during your visit to Key West for local island fare, this restaurant is like no other. Formerly a pool hall, Blue Heaven started in 1989 with one picnic table. The atmosphere is ultra-"Key West" and laid-back with indoor and outdoor seating options. Live music is usually featured at night on the weekends. You will even find chickens roaming the grounds. We ate a late lunch on a bright blue picnic table with sunflowers painted on the top. But don't let the atmosphere fool you. The food here is wonderful. A lot of it is made from scratch, including the bread and tartar sauce. The black bean soup is excellent, and the orange juice is fresh squeezed. The drink menu also provides some great options, including the popular "Straight to Heaven" and "Blue Heaven Rum Punch." A fabulous dessert is the Banana Heaven...WOW! Open daily 8:00 A.M.–10:30 P.M.

B.O.'s Fish Wagon

801 Caroline St.; (305) 294-9272

Fast food Key West style; C; $; NR; Lunch, dinner

Sometimes the "run-down shacks" have the best food, and B.O.'s is no exception. Home of the Square Grouper Sandwich, it is highly recommended by the locals. Rachael Ray visited B.O.'s during her trip to Key West. If you want to get genuine Key West flavor, B.O.'s must be on your list for lunch. Great fish sandwiches and fries are their specialty, with some fresh limeade to wash it all down. The décor is "post-hurricane destruction," but it adds to the fun and memories. If you don't like wild chickens, go somewhere else. Also recommended are the deep-fried hot dogs on Cuban buns. Open 11:00 A.M.–8:00 P.M. daily.

The Café

509 Southard St.; (305) 296-5515

Vegetarian; C; $$; NR; Lunch, dinner

A mostly vegetarian restaurant, this café makes up with food what it lacks in atmosphere. The healthy fare is always a hit with both vegetarians and non-vegetarians alike. Beer and wine are also served here. Open for lunch and dinner 11:00 A.M.–10:00 P.M.; closed Sundays.

Café Marquesa

600 Fleming St.; (305) 292-1244
www.marquesa.com

Contemporary American; C; $$$–$$$$; S; Dinner

Celebrity Chef Susan Ferry, who was trained by Chef Norman Van Aken, makes her home at Key West's own Café Marquesa. Offering contemporary American cuisine, this café is highly recommended by the locals and has received numerous awards. The theme of the restaurant is "Food of the Americas," and there is something for everyone. The menu tends to be pricier than those of other restaurants, but it is worth it for an exceptional dining experience. It also features a cool wine bar. Be sure to make reservations. Dinner daily 6:00 P.M.–11:00 P.M.

Café Sole

1029 Southard St.; (305) 294-0230
www.cafesole.com

French/seafood fusion; C; $$$; S; Lunch, dinner

Highly recommended by the locals and rated the #1 restaurant in the Florida Keys by Zagat in 2004, this place is definitely worth the walk off Duval Street. We had Chef Correa's award-winning Hog Snapper, made with a roasted red pepper zabaglione. We also indulged in the Conch Carpaccio. Although the menu features a vast array of fish dishes, land lovers will also enjoy lamb, duck, and steak options. Chef Correa studied in France and has brought a piece of the fabulous country to Key West. Great service, beer, and wine are all found here, as well as indoor or outdoor dining. Open daily 11:00 A.M.–2:30 P.M. for lunch and 5:30 P.M.–10:00 P.M. for dinner.

Camille's Restaurant

1202 Simonton St.; (305) 296-4811
www.camilleskeywest.com

"Exotic family cooking with No Boundaries"; C; $; S; Breakfast, lunch, dinner

This funky diner-like restaurant offers breakfast, lunch, and dinner and was voted best breakfast in the U.S. by AOL and Zagat. Known for its gourmet dining on a budget, Camille's offers what is described as an "orgy" of breakfast options, including Yellow Corn Cashew Waffles topped with fresh mango/passion fruit and coconut milk sauce, Decadent French Toast with Godiva white chocolate sauce, fresh strawberries, buttermilk pancakes with our favorite Capt. Morgan Spiced Rum Bananas Foster sauce, and three-egg omelet with fresh lobster, asparagus, brie cheese, and diced tomatoes. Dinner options are described as "orgasmic" and range from filet mignon to veal to crab claws. Camille's key lime pie is reputedly the island's finest and was name "Best Key Lime Pie in the World" by Zagat. A favorite of both locals and tourists. Open daily 8:00 A.M.–3:00 P.M. and 6:00–10:00 P.M.

Caroline's

310 Duval St.; (305) 294-7511

Island fare; C; $$; NR; Lunch, dinner

A quaint spot located on Duval, Caroline's offers decent portions of local fare. The key lime pie is awesome, with a layer of chocolate on the bottom. Popular items include the Conch Fritters, Southwest Chicken Salad, and the Skirt Steak. Seating is limited. Open daily 11:00 A.M.–10:00 P.M.

Cheeseburger Key West

217 Duval St.; (305) 296-9466

Burgers; C; $; NR; Breakfast, lunch, dinner

This chain of burger joints was started by two women in Hawaii. Here you can find all types of burgers available at any time. After a few days of seafood, we were ready for a burger, and this place hit the spot. We tasted the house specialty, which was cooked to perfection, with a tasty bun and wonderful sauce. They offer great drinks and live music Wednesday through Sunday evenings. Open daily 8:00 A.M.–11:00 P.M.

Commodore Waterfront

700 Front St.; (305) 294-9191
www.commodorekeywest.com

American/Seafood; C; $$$; NR; Dinner

With an amazing view of the Historic Seaport, Commodore offers delectable seafood and juicy steaks, along with appetizers such as Lobster Cocktail and Tuna Tataki. Make reservations if you are interested in sitting on the private balcony overlooking the water. Although it is more upscale than most places in Key West, you will still see casual attire. This place is also great for private parties and boasts a wonderful wine list. Don't forget to try the Chocolate Sin for dessert. Free parking is available at 700 Front Street. Dinner served daily beginning at 5:30 P.M.

Where to Eat ◆ 55

Conch Republic Seafood Company

631 Greene St. (Key West Harbor); (305) 294-4403
www.conchrepublicseafood.com

Seafood; C; $-$$; NR; Lunch, dinner, late night

A great place for drinks and food, it used to be an old fish house (you'll notice the big bays facing the water) in the historic seaport. In addition to great seafood and seaport grub, it offers a very casual, laid-back atmosphere that lends itself well to parties and celebrations. Guests enjoy watching the four 16-gallon saltwater fish tanks that display beautiful marine life.

Conch Shop

308 Petronia St.; (305) 294-4140

Island fare; C; $; NR; Breakfast, lunch, dinner, late night

Looking for real Key West cuisine? Then look no further than the Conch Shop. Owner Patrick's father started making conch in 1939, and the family business continues. Although the dining is mostly take-out, locals flock here for the morning special of boiled fish and grits. Other options include the "Nasty Burger"; fried ham; and lettuce, tomato, and French fry sandwich. Hours: Thursday to Saturday 5:00 P.M.–midnight; Sunday 8:00 A.M.–1:00 P.M.

Croissants de France

816 Duval St.; (305) 294-2624
www.croissantsdefrance.com

French; C; $-$$: NR; Breakfast, brunch, lunch

Despite experiencing a devastating fire on Valentine's Day 2005, Croissants continues to serve some of the finest baked goods found on the island, which are all made with pure creamy butter and other natural ingredients. Be sure to try the gallettes, quiches, crepes, brioche sandwiches, and, of course, the wonderful croissants. Closed on Wednesdays.

Damn Good Food To-Go

700 Front St.; (305) 294-0011
www.damngoodfoodtogo.com

A great place to pick up food on the go, DGF is located at the A&B Marina at the Historic Seaport Harborwalk. It offers some patio seating and is an ideal stop for picking up food prior to your water excursions. Options range from breakfast favorites, muffins and pastries, salads, deli-style sandwiches, cold house specialties (e.g., chicken, tuna salad), hot house specialties (e.g., Cubans, burritos, BBQ), rotisserie chicken, grilled favorites, dinner sides, appetizers, coffee, and desserts. The merchandise is fun, too! Be sure to ask about the daily specials. Hours: 6:00 A.M.–midnight daily; delivery: 7:00 A.M.–midnight.

El Siboney Restaurant

900 Catherine St.; (305) 296-4184
www.elsiboneyrestaurant.com

Cuban; C; $; NR; Lunch, dinner

Considered one of the best of Key West's Cuban restaurants by the locals, serving lunch and dinner. Be sure to try the roast pork, piccadillo (ground beef with tomatoes and garlic with rice and beans), and ropa vieja (shredded beef). The restaurant only takes cash, and drinks are limited to beer, sangria, and wine. Open Monday through Saturday, 11:00 A.M.–9:30 P.M.; closed Sunday.

Finnegan's Wake

320 Grinnell St.; (305) 293-0222
www.keywestirish.com

Irish; C; $; NR; Lunch, dinner, late night

Irish restaurant and pub with live Irish entertainment. The menu features potato leek soup, potato pancakes, Irish stew, corned beef and cabbage, and Shepherd's Pie. Beer on tap includes Guinness, Harp, Bass, and Murphy's Stout. Late-night menu available. Open daily 11:00 A.M.–4:00 A.M.

58 ◆ *Girls Getaway Guide to Key West*

Fogarty's Bar & Restaurant

227 Duval St.; (305) 294-7525

American; C; $; NR; Lunch, dinner

Fogarty's features a menu for all with great items such as salads, pastas, seafood, sandwiches, and baskets. You and the girls can dine outside under an umbrella (with misters) or in the air conditioning inside. A full bar is available (Flying Monkey), and the most popular cocktail is undoubtedly the piña colada. All frozen drinks are $6, and you can have ringside seats for the Duval Pub Crawl. Open daily 11:00 A.M.–1:00 A.M.

Hard Rock Café

313 Duval St.; (305) 293-0230
www.hardrock.com

American; C; $$; NR; Lunch, dinner

The smallest of all Hard Rock's, the Key West location is housed in an 11,000-square-foot, three-story Victorian mansion that is now the 57th location for the café chain. It features the typical fare of hamburgers, fried shrimp, T-shirts, and celebrity memorabilia, and visitors can dine inside or outside. Open weekdays 11:00 A.M.–11:00 P.M.; weekends 11:00 A.M.–midnight.

Harpoon Harry's

832 Caroline St.; (305) 294-8744

Greasy spoon; C; $; NR; Breakfast, lunch

Any local who knows and loves breakfast (or lunch for that matter) has Harpoon Harry's up on the list of favorites. One block from the Historic Seaport, this "greasy spoon" is an excellent diner with some of the friendliest staff around. Open daily 6:30 A.M.–3:00 P.M.

Hot Tin Roof

0 Duval St. (Ocean Key Resort); (305) 296-7701
www.oceankey.com

Conch fusion; C/D; $$$; S; Breakfast, dinner

Housed on the second floor of the Ocean Key Resort, the "conch fusion" offerings typify unique, Key West-inspired cuisine. The restaurant offers an elegant harbor view dining room so guests can enjoy their meal with a view of the sunset. They often have live jazz music. Dishes to die for are the seafood paella and the chocolate lava cake. Open for breakfast 7:30 A.M.–11:30 A.M. and dinner 6:00 P.M.–10:00 P.M.

Islescapes Dinner Cruise

Schooner Wharf (Pier 1, Slip 3); (305) 923-3319
www.islescapes.com

American; C/D; $$$$, R; Lunch, dinner

Enjoy this three-hour cruise (much nicer than Gilligan's) and eat lunch or dinner aboard a fully restored 33-foot motor yacht that departs from historic Key West Harbor. Choose either a gourmet dinner and sunset cruise or a snorkel and lunch; each costs about $95 per person for up to six people. Reservations are required.

Kelly's Caribbean Bar, Grill & Brewery

303 Whitehead St.; (305) 293-8484
www.kellyskeywest.com

American; C; $$; NR; Lunch, dinner

Movie star Kelly McGillis (*Top Gun*) and her husband established this restaurant more than 10 years ago. It has several unique features, such as a bar made from an airplane, a brick-floored garden in the back, and an outdoor stage. The building is famous for being the home of Pan American Airlines, as they sold their first tickets from this building in 1927. Great home-brewed beers are available at Kelly's Southernmost Brewery. The grill offers fresh local fish prepared several ways, including Macadamia Encrusted with Banana Rum Butter. With a full bar and a great house special (mound of fried onions), Kelly's is open daily for lunch noon–4:00 P.M. and for dinner 5:00 P.M.–10:00 P.M.

La Te Da

1125 Duval St.; (305) 296-6706
www.lateda.com

American; C; $$; NR; Breakfast, lunch, dinner

Best known for its famous drag queen shows that take place upstairs in the Crystal Room Cabaret, La Te Da provides some of the most interesting staff in Key West. The establishment opened, then closed, then opened again in the early 1980s in a house where, a century earlier, Cuban revolutionary poet José Marti is said to have given stirring balcony speeches. The restaurant offers an elegant ambiance with entrees such as Caribbean Snapper. Great Sunday brunch. Open daily 8:00 A.M.–11:00 P.M.

Latitudes

245 Front St. (Westin Key West Resort & Marina);
(305) 294-4000

American; D; $$$; R; Breakfast, lunch, dinner

Located on Sunset Key, a beautiful seven-acre island you can access by boat from the Westin Marina, Latitudes offers cuisine that is as amazing as the scenery. It is the only restaurant in town with a suggested dress code of "country club casual." Be sure to make reservations for the restaurant and boat. Open daily 8:00 A.M.–10:00 P.M.

La Trattoria Venezia

524 Duval St.; (305) 296-1075
www.latrattoria.us

Italian; C; $$; NR; Dinner

Referred to by the locals as "La Trat," this highly recommended restaurant has been family owned and operated since 1984. It features traditional Italian dishes, a great wine list, a full bar, and excellent service. We had a wonderful meal with dishes ranging from pasta to lamb. For a great extension to the night, head to Virgilio's cocktail lounge (same owners, same building) for late-night drinks and dancing. Open nightly from 6:00 P.M.–11:00 P.M.

Louie's Backyard

700 Waddell Ave.; (305) 294-1061
www.louiesbackyard.com

American; C/D; $$$; Lunch, dinner

Louie's honors are way too many to mention; suffice it to say the restaurant has won most South Florida awards, and the classic revival building home to the restaurant is on the National Register of Historic Places. It features three wooden decks all overlooking the ocean: one under cover with fans, another adjacent to the bar ("The After Deck"), and a third that is oceanfront; all provide a great beachfront setting. Louie's is pricey, but the experience is worth it. I've even heard that Louie's is Jimmy Buffett's late-night hangout when he is in town. Locals rave about the Conch Fritters, and the Conch Chowder is a hit as well. Open daily 11:30 A.M.–3:00 P.M. and 6:00 P.M.–10:30 P.M.

Mangoes

700 Duval St.; (305) 292-4606
www.mangoeskeywest.com

Caribbean; C; $$; NR; Lunch, dinner

With a fantastic view of the wild and wonderful Duval Street in the brick courtyard, Mangoes can provide the ideal Key West dining experience on its "see-and-be-seen patio." Flavor options include Caribbean island treats like coconut, passion fruit, mangoes, yucca, and mojo, and entrée options include mozzarella roulade wrapped in spinach, grilled mahi-mahi on pita with sautéed onions, pepper jack cheese, and tartar sauce. Open daily 11:30 A.M.–midnight.

Martin's Café Restaurant

917 Duval St.; (305) 295-0111
www.martins-restaurant.com

German; C; $$; R; Light lunch, dinner

The menu features a nice eclectic mix of German-meets-island fare. Classically-trained chef Martin Busam provides great authentic German dishes, homemade breads, fabulous desserts, a wonderful wine list, and German draft beers. Martin's also offers a full bar, inside dining, a palm tree garden, lounge, and live entertainment. The bar opens at 2:00 P.M. daily, offering a bar menu for a light lunch. Dinner is served daily starting at 5:30 P.M. Brunch is served Friday through Sunday from 10:00 A.M. –3:00 P.M.

Michaels

532 Margaret St.; (305) 295-1300
www.michaelskeywest.com

Classic/American; C; $$; R; Dinner

Considered by many locals to be one of the best restaurants on the island, Michaels is off Duval in a charming residential area of Old Town. Though small and cozy, it is upscale and fancy, complete with designer martinis, superb service, a fondue bar, wonderful presentation, and an excellent wine list. All beef is prime and flown in from Chicago each day, and the seafood selections change to ensure freshness. Michaels was voted by Zagat as one of the top five restaurants in Key West. I highly recommend the Seafood Crepe—it's amazing—as well as the Pomegranate Martini and The Hemingway Cocktail. Opens daily at 5:30 P.M.

Nine One Five

915 Duval St.; (305) 296-0669
www.915duval.com

Tapas; C; $$; S; Dinner

Looking for a bit of sophistication on Duval? A local-recommended favorite for tapas, this great restaurant is situated in a picturesque Victorian home and provides global lounge music for an ultra-trendy vibe. Unique dishes are favorites here, such as the Tuna Dome, their signature dish of fresh Dungeness crab wrapped in Ahi sashimi drizzled in lemon miso dressing. And we must all indulge in the dessert—Life by Chocolate. Dinner served daily from 6:00 P.M.–11:00 P.M.

Pepe's Café

806 Caroline St.; (305) 294-7192
www.pepescafe.net

American; C; $; NR; Breakfast, lunch, dinner

A legendary landmark that was founded in 1909, Pepe's offers breakfast, lunch, and dinner inside or out. For a casual meal along with a piece of Key West history, complete with picnic tables, visit Pepe's. Be sure to try their amazing blueberry pancakes and a mimosa. Hours: 7:30 A.M.–10:30 P.M.

Pisces

1007 Simonton St.; (305) 294-7100
www.pisceskeywest.com

French Caribbean; $$$–$$$$; R; Dinner

This award-winning French Caribbean boutique restaurant features fabulous food served in an outdoor garden or an indoor dining room decorated with Andy Warhol's art. The signature dish is Lobster Tango Mango. Other favorites include the Yellowtail Atocha and the Raspberry Duck. Pisces offers an extensive wine list and great service. Open daily for dinner 6:00 P.M.–10:00 P.M.

Strip House

1435 Simonton St. (at Reach Resort); (305) 295-9669
www.striphouse.net

American; $$$; R; Breakfast, lunch, dinner

Opened in May 2008 at the Reach Resort, this restaurant provides great views of the Atlantic Ocean and décor featuring deep red walls, soft lighting, and black-and-white photos of 1920s glamour girls. "Rich" is the operative word for Strip House dining: steaks, wine, chocolate, pastas. These fabulous items are sure to delight your taste buds and satisfy your appetite. Portions are large enough for girls to share, and there is no plating charge. Open Sunday to Thursday 5:30 P.M.–10:00 P.M.; Friday and Saturday 5:30 P.M.–11:00 P.M. Breakfast (8:00 A.M.–11:00 A.M.) and lunch (11:30 A.M.–3:00 P.M.) are served on the outside patio with separate menus.

Turtle Kraals Restaurant & Bar

231 Margaret St.; (305) 294-2640
www.turtlekraals.com

American; C; $$; NR; Breakfast, lunch, dinner

Once the site of the first Key West turtle cannery in 1849, it's now a great place to dine with water close by. We had a fantastic lunch here on their dock and were able to watch the boaters come and go. Their breakfast specials are listed as "Eight reasons for you to get out of bed."

Daily lunch options include salads, sandwiches, and great seafood selections. Seafood platters are also popular dinner choices. Be sure to catch the live turtle races every Monday and Friday at 6:00 PM. Hours: Sunday to Thursday 7:00 A.M.–10:00 P.M.; open Friday and Saturday until 10:30 P.M.

Two Friends Patio

512 Front St.; (305) 296-3124
www.twofriendskeywest.com

American; $–$$; NR; Breakfast, lunch, dinner

The name says it all, but of course you can bring more than two friends to this fun karaoke stop. Two Friends is the original Patio Restaurant of Old Town Key West. Established in 1967, it has been a family-owned landmark for more than four decades. Breakfast begins at 8:00 A.M., and an early-bird dinner is served from 4:00 P.M.–7:00 P.M. with prices starting at $9.95. Regular dinner prices are more costly. Food ranges from fish sandwiches to salads to snow crab legs to seafood fettuccine to steaks. Open daily 8:00 A.M.–until...

Willie T's

525 Duval St.; (305) 294-7674
American; C; $; NR; Breakfast, lunch, dinner

This is great place to watch the Duval Street action while indulging in a full bar, indoor/outdoor seating, and live entertainment. There is often a lot of action to watch in the restaurant as well as on the street. There's always a fun vibe here. In fact, the restaurant's sign reads "This is paradise." Willie's T's offers juice and java, breakfast, salads, pizza, wings, burgers, wraps, sandwiches, paninis, pasta, dinner entrees, and vegetarian options.

> *"My weaknesses have always been food and men—in that order."*
>
> —DOLLY PARTON

CHAPTER 5

Where to Get Pampered

Pampering is an essential component to a girls getaway, and Key West has several spas and salons that will help you relax and Leave Your Baggage at Home™. Massages, seaweed wraps, and a sauna…a spa vacation can soothe your soul, heal your body, and unclutter your mind. From resort spas to the locals' favorites, this chapter provides some options to consider for the girls who want to indulge in the ultimate "down time."

"Beauty comes in all sizes—not just size 5."

—ROSEANNE BARR

Aveda's Salon on Duval

429 Caroline St. (corner of Duval); (305) 292-6020
www.salononduval.com

A full-service salon and day spa in Old Town offering hair, makeup, skincare, massage, body treatments, and waxing. Gift certificates available. Specializing in wedding parties and large groups. A Swedish massage is $90 for 60 minutes. Hours: 10:00 A.M.–6:00 P.M.; closed Wednesdays and Sundays.

Caribbean Spa

One Duval; (305) 296-4600 ext. 1010
www.pierhouse.com

One of the best massages I have ever had was at the Caribbean Spa (thanks, John). Although the spa is part of the Pier House, it is a separate building with a parking lot, making it easy for non-hotel guests to experience this great spa. The Caribbean Spa offers the signature Milk and Honey Body Treatment, Mango Mud Massage, and the Caribbean Coma Massage. Open seven days a week from 8:30 A.M.–7:00 P.M. A 50-minute Swedish massage is $95.

Prana Spa

625 Whitehead St.; (305) 295-0100
www.pranaspakeywest.com

Highly recommended by locals, this spa offers all types of massages, including deep tissue, Swedish aromatherapy, stone, and Thai yoga. All types of skincare are also provided with the Age Reversing and Firming Facial, a favorite. Other treatments clients opt for are Body Scrubs, after-sun and sunburn treatments, and foot treatments. A 60-minute deep tissue or Swedish massage begins at $95. Open Monday to Saturday 11:00 A.M.–7:00 P.M.; Sunday 11:00 A.M.–5:00 P.M.

Where to Get Pampered ◆ 71

The Solar Spa

2824 N. Roosevelt Blvd.; (305) 295-7177
www.thesolarspa.com

Massages, peels, wax, tanning, Botox, microdermabrasion, permanent cosmetics, collagen injections, manicures, and pedicures are offered here. Relax in the lavender and eucalyptus aroma-filled steam room before you have your treatment. A 60-minute Swedish massage is $80. Open Monday to Saturday 10:00 A.M.–7:00 P.M.; Sunday 10:00 A.M.–5:00 P.M.

SpaTerre—Ocean Key Resort & Spa

Zero Duval St.; (305) 295-7017
www.oceankey.com

Offering Balinese spa treatments and Thai body rituals that provide total relaxation through body wraps, massages, facials, manicures, and pedicures, SpaTerre also provides couples massages and poolside treatments. A 50-minute Swedish massage is $100. Hours: 8:00 A.M.–8:00 P.M. daily.

CHAPTER 6

Where to Find Galleries, Museums, and Nature Attractions

Key West serves as a melting pot for art and nature lovers, so it is no surprise that art galleries and natural attractions are very popular on the island. Couple that with Key West's rich and exciting history and you have interesting and unique museums to explore. From photography to contemporary art to woodworking to sculptures to jewelry, Key West's art galleries provide a vast array of media and styles to explore. The nature attractions highlight Key West's fantastic biodiversity and beauty. The museums house artifacts ranging from pirate and sunken treasures to the works of famous Key West personalities such as Ernest Hemingway, Robert Frost, and Harry S. Truman.

74 ◆ *Girls Getaway Guide to Key West*

Galleries

7 Artists Gallery

604 Duval St.; (305) 293-0411
www.7artistskeywest.com

Opened in December 2002, this quintessential Key West arts and crafts gallery features works from seven of the island's most respected artists. Works include sculptures, paintings, jewelry, and much more. A great gallery with fantastic items for souvenirs or gifts to take home.

Open daily 10:00 A.M.–10:00 P.M.

Alan S. Maltz Gallery

1210 Duval St.; (305) 294-0005
www.alanmaltz.com

Dubbed "The Original Wildlife Photographer in the State of Florida," Maltz is an award-winning photographer who established this gallery in 1999. His coffee table books *Key West Color* and *Miami: City of Dreams* rank among the finest in their genre. A world-class photographer, Maltz has had work featured in places such as the Ritz Carlton-St. Thomas, Southwest Florida International Airport, Carnival Cruise Lines, and American Airlines Arena.

Open daily 10:00 A.M.–6:00 P.M.

Where to Find Galleries, Museums, and Nature Attractions ◆ 75

Archeo Gallery

1208 Duval St.; (305) 294-3771
www.archeogallery.com

This unique gallery features ancient art for your modern lifestyle, including rugs, furniture, and art. The vibrant tribal Gabbeh rugs are made of handspun wool and knotted by nomads. The handmade teak "village furniture" is from the island of Java, and each piece in unique. The gallery also houses ceremonial art from Africa, including masks, sculptures, metals, and pottery. You are sure to find some interesting items.

Open Monday to Saturday 10:00 A.M.–6:00 P.M.; Sunday noon–5:00 P.M.

A Boy and His Dog

826 Duval St.; (305) 296-7721
626 Duval St.; (305) 296-5527
www.aboyandhisdog.net

Due to its popularity, the owners (David Miller and his dog Simon, a Dalmatian/Chow mix) had to expand to a second location only a block away. My favorite pieces are Thomas Arvid's wonderful wine paintings and Michael Flohr's city scene paintings.

Open daily 10:30 A.M.–10:00 P.M.

Charest-Weinberg Gallery

1111 Duval St.; (305) 292-0411
www.charest-weinberg.com

Housed in a wonderfully restored, century-old building, this gallery opened in 2005. It features work by local artists as well as internationally–renowned artists. It also features other art-related services, including framing, international shipping, and consultation on everything from art acquisition to installation to collection management. The gallery offers rental space for private parties and special events. Be sure to visit the gallery's website for shows and other happenings.

Open daily 10:00 A.M.–6:00 P.M.

East Martello Museum and Gallery

3501 S. Roosevelt Blvd.; (305) 296-3913

If you have heard about Robert the Doll, you must stop by and say hello to him. In addition to Robert, several locally-created or themed art exhibits are housed here each year, which often coincide with other cultural activities. The gallery is located in a series of arched rooms in a mid-19th-century brick fort. The outdoor garden and upstairs in the second and third levels of the citadel are the magnificent and zany metal sculptures of welder and junk-sculptor Stanley Papio.

Open daily 9:30 A.M.–4:30 P.M.

Where to Find Galleries, Museums, and Nature Attractions ◆ 77

Gallery Key West

824 Duval St.; (305) 292-0046

An eclectic collection of fine art and home furnishings created by local artists Pam Hobbs, Christine Black, Janis Childs, Egg, Wayne Smith, Lynne Fischer, Elizabeth Calleja, and Jessica Wilson. These artists feature colorful and island-made original paintings, sculptures, pottery, and jewelry.

Open daily 10:00 A.M.–10:00 P.M.

Gallery on Greene

606 Greene St.; (305) 294-1669
www.galleryongreene.com

This gallery features a collection of area artists, including a series of Mario Sanchez originals signed by the artist, who recently passed away at the age of 96. Also represented is Pulitzer Prize-winning cartoonist Jeff MacNelly, who was the creator of the comic strip *Shoe* and a frequent Key West visitor.

Open daily 10:00 A.M.–6:00 P.M.

Gingerbread Square Gallery

1207 Duval St.; (305) 296-8900
www.gingerbreadsquaregallery.com

Founded in 1974 by the late Richard Heyman, North America's first openly gay mayor, this is the oldest gallery in Key West. It currently features beautiful works of tropical scenes as well as flora and fauna by artists such as Jim Salem, John Kiraly, and Michael Palmer. Also on display are art and glass sculptures.

Open weekdays 10:00 A.M.–6:00 P.M.; weekends 10:00 A.M.–10:00 P.M.

Glass Reunions

825 Duval St.; (305) 294-1720
www.glassreunions.com

Look for the mosaic car at Duval and Olivia and you will find Glass Reunions. Voted the #4 retailer of American crafts and representing the works of more than 200 American artists, the gallery features a great collection of all-American glass art, jewelry, kaleidoscopes, paperweights, perfume bottles, lamps, and unique decorative pieces. Complimentary gift wrapping as well as special shipping and orders are available.

Open daily 10:00 A.M.–10:00 P.M.

Guild Hall

614 Duval St.; (305) 296-6076
www.guildhallgallerykw.com

A 27-year-old, two-tiered artists' cooperative, this building was built in 1919 and restored in 1975 by seven women artists. The stairs and railings are from a dismantled Catholic convent, and the floor bricks were salvaged from original Key West streets. Works on display include watercolors, acrylic/mixed media, clay, sculpture, wood, photography, painted ceramics, fused and stained glass, fish rubbings, glass beads, and jewelry.

Open daily 9:30 A.M.–11:00 P.M.

Haitian Art Company

600 Frances St.; (305) 296-8932
www.haitian-art-co.com

Opened in 1978 by the father-daughter team of Boris and Ruth Kravitz, this gallery features oil paintings, folk art, and sculptures that are purchased directly from Haitian artists, helping them to survive in their native country. This artwork tends to be primitive and honest. Papier mâché fish, spirit flags, and animals painted in bright acrylics are fun and affordable. The Haitian Art Company has maintained close ties with many of Haiti's best-known artists and has been instrumental in supporting emerging talent.

Open daily 10:00 A.M.–6:00 P.M.

Hands On

1206 Duval St.; (305) 296-7399
Handsongallery.com

A quaint gallery located in a "Conch" house in the historic area of town features one-of-a-kind pieces of hand-woven wearable art by artisan weaver Ellen Steininger, as well as jewelry and crafts. Featured artists provide a wide range of styles, clothes, and accessories, including purses, belts, scarves, and shawls.

Open daily 10:00 A.M.–6:00 P.M.

Harrison Gallery

825 White St.; (305) 294-0609
www.harrison-gallery.com

For more than 20 years, Harrison has been owned and operated by wood sculptor Helen Harrison, who turned to woodwork after she and her husband, musician/writer Ben Harrison (*Undying Love*) built the 38-foot sailboat they lived in and sailed on for 11 years. That boat brought them to Key West from Costa Rica. From scraps of mahogany, walnut, and sea hibiscus wood, Helen creates her richly grained and wood-colored sculptures.

The gallery also features a wide variety of unusual artwork from oils to bronze to mirrors to painted shutters. Helen has a talent for finding unique pieces to feature in her gallery.

Open Monday to Saturday noon–5:00 P.M.

Helio Gardens Gallery

526 Angela St.; (305) 294-7901
www.heliographics.com

The gallery is located in the Gardens Hotel, where the lush atmosphere is a perfect complement to the art on display. Owner Dawn Wilkins features colorful botanical and fruit-themed paintings, ceramics, photographs, wood frames, and textiles (pillows, fabrics, shirts), mostly created by local artists. A percentage of the profits benefits organizations working to save the reefs and to support the arts.

Open daily noon–5:00 P.M.

Island Arts Co-op

1128 Duval St.; (305) 292-9909
www.island-arts.com

Twenty Key West and Lower Keys artists show their Caribbean-style work at this gallery, which features affordable prints, paintings, crafts, sculptures, stained-glass mosaics, unique frames, jewelry, photography, watercolors, acrylics, iron, copper, bronze, ceramics, and glass.

Open daily 9:00 A.M.–9:00 P.M.

Joy Gallery

1124 Duval St.; (305) 296-3039

A Key West landmark with more than 10 years on the art scene, this gallery features fine art at affordable prices, including originals by local and international artists.

Open Monday to Saturday 10:00 A.M.–6:00 P.M.

Kennedy Gallery

511 Duval St.; (305) 294-3039

The owners of this gallery and framing emporium (which is no longer associated with its founder, Robert Kennedy) believe art should be moderately priced and available to everyone. Here you will find some very nice toilet art, such as painted toilet seats. Also, be sure to check out the curvy furniture and caliches oils on canvas. Ask about the gallery's very reasonable framing service.

Open daily 10:00 A.M.–10:00 P.M.

Kent Gallery

821 Duval St.; (305) 292-5646
www.kentgalleryart.com

A contemporary art gallery that focuses on 21st-century mid-career and emerging visual artists, it was originally founded as an art center by F. Morgan Townsend, who came to Key West to work for President Franklin Roosevelt's Works Progress Administration in 1933. It is currently owned and managed by Claire Kent and features rugs and chandeliers in addition to fine art.

Open daily 10:00 A.M.–5:00 P.M.

Key West Gallery

601 Duval St.; (305) 292-9339
www.keywestartgalleries.com

Michael Berry and Kellie Alpert specialize in investment originals, collectible hand-embellished limited editons, Murano Glass, and selected bronze work.

The invitingly big-windowed gallery carries some of Hawaiian seascape specialist Roy Gonzalez Tabora's work as well as a wide variety of international talent. The gallery boasts artists from three continents.

Open daily 10:00 A.M.–10:00 P.M.

KW Light Gallery

1203 Duval St.; (305) 294-0566
www.kwlightgallery.com

Writer, photographer, and painter Sharon Wells offers her contemporary works, including fine art giclée prints and prints of historic Key West photographs. The gallery also features Key West, Cuba, international, and cemetery art.

Open daily 10:00 A.M.–6:00 P.M.

Lucky Street Gallery

1130 Duval St.; (305) 294-3973

With a focus on contemporary fine art, Dianne Zolotow moved her bright gallery from White Street to the uptown end of Duval. She has been featuring talented local artists for many years. The gallery offers new shows every two weeks.

Open Monday to Saturday 11:00 A.M.–6:00 P.M.

Luis Sottil Gallery

716 Duval St.; (305) 292-6447
www.luissottil.com

The signature artist, Luis Sottil, is the creator of "naturalismo," a system of painting with natural ingredients like 14K gold paint. Sottil shares proceeds from his wild animals and insect paintings with needy kids with cancer or HIV. This is a wonderful gallery with other interesting items, including acrylic-based sculptures by artist Bill Mack, plus works by other world-renowned artists, all of whom frequently visit this gallery.

Open Sunday to Thursday 10:00 A.M.–10:00 P.M.; Friday and Saturday 10:00 A.M.–11:00 P.M.

Mary O'Shea's Glass Garden

213 Simonton St.; (305) 293-8822
www.maryosheasglassgarden.com

The largest glass studio gallery in the Florida Keys includes everything from dishes to fishes, art glass, dinnerware, jewelry, paintings, and sculptures.

Open Monday to Saturday 10:00 A.M.–5:00 P.M.

Oh My Godard Gallery

719 Duval St.; (305) 292-0911

The gallery boasts that Michael Godard is the top-selling artist in the world. His paintings and reproductions feature martini glasses, dancing olives, poker chips, and other artifacts of the high life. Ironically, Godard does not drink himself. Not your typical gallery, it features a stripper pole in the front window and loud rock 'n' roll music playing throughout. Definitely an experience!

Open daily 10:00 A.M.–10:00 P.M.

Red Door Gallery

812 Caroline St.; (305) 296-6628

For more than 20 years, this gallery, located across from the Waterfront Market, has been the spot to buy affordable island and Caribbean-inspired artwork as well as colorful Key West scenery creations by local artists and owner René Blais.

Open daily 10:00 A.M.–10:00 P.M.

Senses at Play Exotic Fine Art Gallery

1214 Laird St.; (305) 294-5008
www.sensesatplay.com

A unique gallery featuring exotic and erotic photographs. The owners, John and Bernadette McCall, are photographers for hire and can be commissioned. After the photography session, they can then create a portrait on print, canvas, or tiles or assemble a sentimental album.

By appointment only.

Sign of Sandford

328 Simonton St.; (305) 296-7493
www.signofsandford.com

You will find owner/artist Sandford Birdsey busy here in her shop painting in watercolors, designs, and hand-paints fabric and splashing color on silk scarves, furniture, and anything else that will hold paint. This gallery hosts the Paint Key West, an annual outdoor painting workshop hosted and conducted by Sandford herself.

Open Monday to Saturday 10:00 A.M.–6:00 P.M.

Stone Soup Gallery

519 Fleming St.; (305) 296-2080

An eclectic gallery and frame shop, it features the art of David Klein, Kate Peachey, and several Cuban artists.

Open Tuesday to Saturday 10:00 A.M.–5:00 P.M.

Suzy Starfish

912 Duval St.; (305) 292-6624
Suzystarfish.com

If you like bright artwork, then plan to visit Suzy Starfish, which showcases lamps, vases, and jewelry in vivid colors. The store is best known for its cheerful artwork depicting all types of tropical fauna, including fish, parrots, cats, dogs, and iguanas. A great place to buy gifts.

Open Tuesday to Sunday 10:00 A.M.–6:00 P.M.

Thomas Kinkade

335 Duval St., Suite E; (305) 292-0069
www.thomaskinkade.com

This Duval Street gallery is home to the work of America's most collected living artist, Thomas Kinkade, the "Painter of Light." Kinkade emphasizes simple pleasures and inspirational messages through his paintings. He has been nationally recognized for his art as well as his philanthropic endeavors.

Open daily 10:00 A.M.–7:00 P.M.

Wings of Imagination

1316 Duval St.; (305) 296-2988
www.wingsofimagination.com

A part of The Key West Butterfly & Nature Conservatory, the gift shop can be visited separately from the butterfly habitat. For all things butterfly and nature-related, stop by this store, which is filled with garden, gift, and home items, all influenced by the butterfly.

Open weekdays 10:00 A.M.–6:00 P.M.; weekends 10:00 A.M.–10:00 P.M.

Wyland Galleries of Key West

623 Duval St.; (305) 292-4998
102 Duval St.; (305) 292-5240
www.wylandkw.com

With two locations in Key West, Wyland is recognized as the world's leading marine life artist practicing in both paint and sculpture. These galleries also feature work by many other contemporary artists. Wyland uses his work to raise awareness about the need to protect the oceans and their creatures. For moving art depictions of marine life, stop by Wyland.

Open daily 10:00 A.M.–10:00 P.M.

Zbyszek Gallery

1102 Duval St.; (305) 296-8030
www.zbyszek.com

With a quote from *Alice in Wonderland* on the website, Zbyszek loves to project imagery via abstract, surreal sculptures and wearable art created by the husband-and-wife team of Zbyszek and Tippi Koziol. They have been the owners and resident artists of this gallery for more than 10 years. Here you can find digital art, T-shirts, wood plaques, plaques and prints, and paintings.

Open daily 10:30 A.M.–6:00 P.M.

> *"My life has a brilliant cast, but I can't figure out the plot."*
> —ASHLEIGH BRILLIANT

Museums

Audubon House & Tropical Gardens

205 Whitehead St.; (305) 294-2116
www.audubonhouse.com

A glimpse into mid-19th-century life on the island is offered at the Audubon House, which provides an exploration into local history and folklore, as well as a lush one-acre tropical garden and stunning antiques. Visitors will see the works of John James Audubon, a world-renowned ornithologist, as there are 28 first-edition Audubon works in the house. An audio tour is available. Admission is $10. Open every day from 9:30 A.M.–5:00 P.M. Visit the website for discount coupon.

Ernest Hemingway Home & Museum

907 Whitehead St.; (305) 294-1136
www.hemingwayhome.com

Between 1931 and 1940, legendary American writer Ernest "Papa" Hemingway (1899–1961) lived in this Spanish colonial-style house built from coral rock. While here, he wrote many of his most famous works, including *Death in the Afternoon*, *To Have and Have Not*, and *For Whom the Bell Tolls*. Remnants of his life there include his portraits, furniture, prized boxing gloves, and descendants of his six-toed cats. A Hemingway expert leads the tour of the home and surrounding grounds and provides many humorous and interesting stories about the author. General adult admission is $12. Open every day from 9:00 A.M.–5:00 P.M.

Harry S. Truman Little White House

111 Front St.; (305) 294-9911
www.trumanlittlewhitehouse.com

As the winter White House of America from 1946–1952 and still used by high-ranking government officials today, the Harry S. Truman Little White House is a unique historic site. See where presidents relaxed and how they spent their time. Tour guides introduce visitors to the personal side of the Harry S. Truman presidency as well as provide a glimpse into the politics of the Cold War and the naval history of Key West. The house is open daily, and tours are offered every 20 minutes from 9:00 A.M.– 4:30 P.M. Admission is $12 for adults.

Key West Heritage House Museum & Robert Frost Cottage

410 Caroline St.; (305) 296-3573
www.heritagehousemuseum.org

This unique museum represents nearly 200 years of Key West culture, as you will see through the lives of the Porter family, who lived on the island for seven generations. Built in the 1830s, the Caribbean Colonial house was last occupied by Jessie Porter, an avid preservationist who has been dubbed the island's "grand dame of hospitality."

The Annual Robert Frost Poetry Festival is typically held in April each year and brings notable poets as well as art and film to the area. The self-guided tour of historic homes along the Pelican Path include this home, the Audubon House, and The Oldest House for $15 admission.

Open 10:00 A.M.–4:00 P.M. daily; closed Sundays.

90 ◆ *Girls Getaway Guide to Key West*

Key West Museum of Art & History

281 Front St. (The Custom House); (305) 295-6616
www.kwahs.com

Built in 1891, the Custom House is one of south Florida's most important historic buildings and served, at one time, as Key West's Court House. A recently-completed nine-year, $9 million restoration project brought the red brick building back to life. It is now home to the Key West Art and Historical Society, which draws upon its extensive collection of art and artifacts to present changing exhibits featuring Key West's history and rich artistic heritage. During one of my visits, a celebrity bronze, life-sized sculpture exhibit from J. Seward Johnson and a great Ernest Hemingway photo and story display were featured. The Custom House was recognized in *Florida Monthly Magazine* as Florida's Best Renovated Building, Best Historical Landmark, and Best Museum.

Open daily 9:00 A.M.–5:00 P.M.

Key West Shipwreck Historeum Museum

1 Whitehead St.; (305) 292-8990
www.shipwreckhistoreum.com

Return to the Key West of 1851, where you'll find the treacherous world of shipwrecking and how it made Key West the richest city in the U.S. Live actors, artifacts, laser technology, and a 60-foot lookout tower make this a unique experience. Via this self-guided tour, visitors will see a video about the shipwrecking industry, which features interviews, film clips, and underwater footage. You will also see the treasures from the wrecks of the *Isaac Allerton* and other ships. Hours: 9:40 A.M.–5:00 P.M. daily. Last show 4:40 P.M. Admission is $11.

Lighthouse & Keepers Quarters Museum

938 Whitehead St.; (305) 295-6616 ext. 16
www.kwahs.com/lighthouse.htm

Built in 1847, Key West's lighthouse was capable of beaming light 25 miles out to sea. The tower and nearby Keeper's Quarters have been restored and are maintained as they were before the lighthouse was deactivated in 1969. This light station was built after the hurricane of 1846 destroyed the original 1825 tower on the coast. It is the 15th oldest surviving lighthouse in the country. Climb the 88-step circular stairway to enjoy panoramic seascapes and views of the towns. Hours: 9:30 A.M.–4:30 P.M. daily; closed Christmas. Admission is $10/adult.

Mel Fisher Maritime Heritage Society & Museum

200 Greene St.; (305) 294-2633
www.melfisher.org

This museum is dedicated to those interested in sunken treasure and the equipment that has been used to retrieve it. Most impressive are the gold artifacts from 17th-century Spanish galleons, as well as the Mel Fisher story. Here you can see *Atocha* and *Santa Margarita* artifacts (circa 1622), including a 77.777 karat emerald and other beautiful jewelry. Open weekdays 8:30 A.M.–5:00 P.M. Open weekends and holidays 9:30 A.M.–5:00 P.M. Adult admission is $12.

Pat Croce's Pirate Soul Museum

524 Front St.; (305) 292-1113
www.piratesoul.com

An American entrepreneur, author, and TV personality, Pat Croce opened this $10 million museum in January 2005. The museum features authentic pirate artifacts, many from Croce's personal collection, including the world's only authenticated pirate treasure chest and one of two authenticated pirate flags in the world. In February 2006 Croce opened the pirate-themed Rum Barrel restaurant next to the museum. On the 19th of each month, this pirate-themed museum provides free "Grog" (pirates' alcoholic beverage of choice) during your tour. See all aspects of pirate life and hear the tales of the high seas during your guided tour. Hours: 9:00 A.M.–7:00 P.M. daily. Admission is $13.95.

Ripley's Believe It or Not! Key West

108 Duval St.; (305) 293-9939
www.ripleyskeywest.com

As you explore more than 500 exhibits and 8,000 square feet, you will see all sorts of crazy things to...believe it or not! See the car made from 10,000 dimes or the white buffalo. You decide what is real in this wacky museum. Visit the website for a discount coupon.

Hours: 8:30 A.M.–11:00 P.M. daily. Adult admission is $14.95.

Nature & Wildlife Attractions

Florida Keys Eco-Discovery Center

35 E. Quay Rd. (at the end of Southard St. in Truman Annex); (305) 809-4750

www.homeandabroad.com/c/42/Site/79259_Florida_Keys_Eco_Discovery_Center_visit.html

Opened in January 2007, this 6,400-square-foot center provides interactive exhibits highlighting the rich natural environmental of the Florida Keys. Visitors of all ages can learn more about this complex and interesting ecosystem and see the Mote Marine Laboratory's Living Reef Exhibit. Open Tuesday to Saturday 9:00 A.M.–4:00 P.M. Admission is free.

Key West Aquarium

1 Whitehead St.; (305) 296-2051
www.keywestaquarium.com

Want to pet a live shark? Visit the very first tourist attraction in Key West that provides indoor and outdoor exhibits of native Key West marine life as well as a live Touch Tank. Tours and shark feedings occur daily at 11:00 A.M., 1:00 P.M., 3:00 P.M., and 4:30 P.M. Hours: 10:00 A.M.–6:00 P.M. daily. Adult admission is $11.

94 ◆ *Girls Getaway Guide to Key West*

The Key West Butterfly & Nature Conservatory

1316 Duval St.; (305) 296-2988
www.keywestbutterfly.com

After viewing an educational video about butterflies, visitors can take a leisurely stroll through the amazing butterfly environment, where they will see 50 to 60 different butterfly species in a glass-enclosed habitat. The lush area is absolutely beautiful, with gorgeous flowers, gardens, flowing water, wooden bridges, and butterfly-shaped iron benches. You never know which butterfly will land on you and join you through this self-guided tour. Hours: 9:00 A.M.–5:00 P.M. Adult admission is $10.

CHAPTER 7

Where to Find Nightlife

Key West is known for its nightlife and bars, which are predominantly located along the main drag, Duval Street. Key West is located in Monroe County, which encompasses all of the Keys. There are 300 liquor licenses in Monroe County; of those, 200 are in Key West. That should give you an idea of how serious this town is about its nightlife. In Key West you can typically find live music and a great time to suit anyone's taste. This chapter highlights it all from martini/wine bars to salsa to laid-back to country to clothing-optional to drag queen shows.

"Between two evils, I always pick the one I never tried before."

—MAE WEST

801 Bourbon Bar and Cabaret

801 Duval St.; (305) 296-1992
www.801Bourbon.com

If you're walking (or in my case riding a bike), it is hard to miss the loud music and array of drag queens or men dancing on stage. If you stop to watch, you will be beckoned to come inside one of Key West's most popular gay bars as well as the pub across the street. The nightly drag shows are a must-see for those looking for a true Key West experience. The well-known drag queen Sushi makes regular appearances here. Shows nightly at 9:00 P.M. and 11:00 P.M.

Afterdeck Bar and Louie's Backyard

700 Waddell St.; (305) 294-1061
www.louiesbackyard.com

A well-known late-night hangout for Jimmy Buffet when he's in town, Louie's beachside restaurant becomes a cool, laid-back bar at night.

Captain Tony's Saloon

428 Greene St.; (305) 294-1838
www.capttonyssaloon.com

Home of the original Sloppy Joe's, this famous Key West bar was a favorite hangout of Ernest Hemingway and where he met his third wife in 1936. Captain Tony took over the bar in 1958 and sold it again in 1990. Despite being more than 90 years old, Captain Tony still makes frequent appearances at the bar to tell his tales and flirt with any and all of the ladies.

Where to Find Nightlife ◆ 97

Cowboy Bill's Honky Tonk

610 ½ Duval St.; (305) 292-1887
www.cowboybillskw.com

Key West finally got a country bar, which features the island's largest dance floor, a mechanical bull, pool tables, darts, 20 TVs, and, of course, steaks and other scrumptious food. Co-owner Irene McDonough makes a special drink exclusive to Cowboy Bill's called the "Piece of Ass."

Fat Tuesday

305 Duval St.; (305) 296-9373
www.fattuesdaykeywest.com

With excellent frozen drinks and each flavor mixed right on the bar wall, this famous Key West establishment provides strong drinks that taste great and will certainly sneak up on you. A favorite is the 190 Octane, which is an orange-flavored slushie made with grain alcohol. Happy hour is from 4:00–7:00 P.M.

Garden of Eden

224 Duval St.; (305) 296-4565

With the Bull & Whistle on the first and second floors, the Garden of Eden is the top floor bar and a "can't miss" in Key West. This hilarious, clothing-optional bar brings out some interesting characters, and any visitor to Key West should at least go upstairs for a visit.

Grand Vin

1107 Duval St.; (305) 296-1020

This charming wine bar and shop offers a daily menu of 20 fine wines, ports, and champagnes hand-picked by owner and wine connoisseur Sean McConnell. Purchase by the bottle, glass, or in a special "flight" combination of three half-glasses in the windows. The wooden wrap-around porch is the perfect spot to uncork a leisurely evening glass. Open Monday to Saturday 11 A.M.–midnight; Sunday noon–midnight.

Green Parrot Bar

601 Whitehead St.; (305) 294-6133
www.greenparrot.com

The first and last bar on U.S. 1 and a favorite local hangout, this dive bar features live entertainment and no cover or minimum. *Playboy Magazine* rates this bar high in terms of live music. Open daily from 10:00 A.M.–4:00 A.M., it is completely open air and typical of how Key West bars used to be.

Hog's Breath Saloon

400 Front St.; (305) 296-4222
www.hogsbreath.com

With the famous slogan, "Hog's breath is better than no breath at all," the original Hog's Breath was founded in Fort Walton Beach, Florida, 30 years ago by an Alabama native who thought drinking was a sport just as important as fishing or sailing. Everyone's welcome in the three bars with seating in or outdoors and live music starting at 1:00 P.M. daily. Hog's Breath is also home of the highly-acclaimed Key West Songwriters' Festival that brings chart-topping American songwriters to Key West each year.

Irish Kevin's

211 Duval St.; (305) 292-1262
www.irishkevins.com

Known for its Guinness-chugging contests, Irish Kevin's is not for the faint of heart. Don't visit if you have to wake up early the next day. I even got roped into partaking in the on-stage tequila guzzling contest once and then sang back-up for the live musician. Open daily from 10:00 A.M.–3:00 A.M.

Island Dogs Bar

505 Front St.; (305) 295-0501

A newer, classic-style bar with a low-key vibe, Dogs Bar features a daily happy hour from 4:00 P.M.–8:00 P.M., live music every afternoon, dancing Thursday to Sunday from 10:00 P.M.–2:00 A.M., a fabulous outdoor patio, and a fun menu of burgers, fries, quesadillas, and much more. This bar has great couch seating if you are lucky enough to find some available.

KWest

705 Duval St.; (305) 292-8500

A more modern club that features a piano lounge, show tunes, go-go, and a fun happy hour, KWest makes everyone, gay or straight, feel right at home. Open until 4:00 A.M.

La Te Da

1125 Duval St.; (305) 296-6706
www.lateda.com

This upscale venue has its own restaurant and hotel. "Guys as Dolls" and other acts are held in the Crystal Room Cabaret, which plays host to a variety of female impersonators singing live to Broadway musicals as well as comedians. Visit the "By George" Piano Bar, the Terrace Bar, or the Crystal Bar.

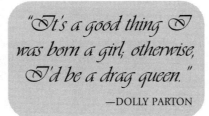

"It's a good thing I was born a girl; otherwise, I'd be a drag queen."
—DOLLY PARTON

Sloppy Joe's Bar

201 Duval St.; (305) 294-5717
www.sloppyjoes.com

Home of the famous "Hemingway Look-a-Like Contest" that takes place each July, this Key West tradition was a favorite of "Papa" Hemingway. With live music and dancing, everyone should stop in Sloppy Joe's for a drink and a world-famous shirt.

Top of La Concha

430 Duval St.; (305) 296-2991
www.laconchakeywest.com

Visit the bar at the top of the La Concha Hotel, a great place for a fabulous drink and an indoor or outdoor panoramic view of Key West. Live music Thursday through Saturday nights. Open daily noon–11:00 P.M.

Where to Find Nightlife ◆ 101

Turtle Kraals Restaurant & Bar

Lands End Village at Key West Bight; (305) 294-2640
www.turtlekraals.com

Great food at this rooftop bar, which offers a sunset view and a large selection of international beers. Live music plays nightly with frequent open-mike nights. Happy hour features oysters by the piece. Open daily noon–11:00 P.M.

Virgilio's

524 Duval St.; (305) 296-1075
www.latrattoria.us

This great martini bar features live music nightly. We caught live salsa music and dancing while we were there. The bar is dark and cozy and offers great martinis. We indulged in the mint chocolate chip and espresso as after-dinner drinks and dessert.

CHAPTER 8

Where to Find Sports, Recreation, and Outdoor Activities

In Key West, there are endless activities that will keep you busy all day long. For adventurers, try parasailing, kayaking, snorkeling, and fishing. For girls looking for a relaxing day, there are sunbathing, yoga, Pilates, sunset cruises, and wine tasting. And for those looking for education and entertainment, be sure to check out the theaters, tours, and historic sites. Undoubtedly, there is something for everyone in Key West.

Beaches

The Beach at Fort Zachary Taylor State Park

Truman Annex; (305) 292-6713

Where the Atlantic Ocean meets the Gulf of Mexico, you'll find one of the Florida Keys' most scenic National Landmarks. This 54-acre park is home to Fort Zachary Taylor, which was completed in 1866 and played an important role in the Civil War and the Spanish-American War. Guided tours of the historic fort are offered daily from October through March. Although history buffs will love the fort, swimmers will enjoy some of the finest snorkeling accessible from shore. You can fish from the rock seawall, wander wooded nature trails, enjoy bird-watching, lunch in a shady picnic area, and watch the boats come through the Key West Ship Channel. Rafts, snorkel gear, floats, chairs, umbrellas, and more are available for rental at the beach at Fort Zach, and there is a food and beverage concession.

Smathers Beach

S. Roosevelt Blvd.

This strip of sand is one of the best-known beaches in Key West. Named after a former governor, it is just west of the airport and, at two miles long, is the island's longest beach. Smathers Beach offers parking, restrooms, concession stands, chair rentals, picnic tables, water sport rentals, and more.

Boating

Key West offers a plethora of boating options: from fishing to waverunner rentals to sailing to kayaking to sunset cruises, your choices are unlimited.

Where to Find Sports, Recreation, and Outdoor Activities ◆ 105

Glass Bottom Boats

Discovery Undersea Tours Key West

www.discoveryunderseatours.com
(800) 262-0099; (305) 293-0099

Passengers can enjoy a narrated tour of a living coral reef on the glass bottom boat *Discovery* while peering through the boat's twenty large windows. A snack bar is on board, seating is available in the sun or shade, and the final excursion of the day is the Champagne Sunset Trip.

Dry Tortugas Trips

Yankee Freedom II

240 Margaret St.; (305) 294-7009
www.yankeefreedom.com

Almost 70 miles west of Key West, nestled among spectacular coral reefs, fascinating shipwrecks, and sandy beaches lie seven undeveloped coral and sand islands called the Dry Tortugas. The Yankee Freedom II, Key West's premier ferry to the Dry Tortugas, departs daily (except Christmas) at 8:00 A.M. Adult prices start at $149/person.

106 ◆ *Girls Getaway Guide to Key West*

Kayaking

Key West Kayaking

(305) 304-0337
www.keyskayakfishing.com

You can leave mornings or afternoons for half or three-quarters day tours to enjoy a kayak snorkel and sail while exploring Key West's unique ecosystem.

Sunset Cruise

Fury Water Adventures

Locations vary; (877) 994-8898
www.furycat.com

Leave your baggage at home™ and onshore as you sail off into Key West's famous sunset aboard a spacious state-of-the-art catamaran. Enjoy and two-hour cruise in the tropical waters of Key West with a warm ocean breeze and a magnificent sunset as a backdrop. Toast the end of another perfect day in paradise as you watch the sun slowly disappear beyond the horizon. Relax and enjoy complimentary beer, wine, champagne, and soda. Adult prices start at $37 (visit the website for discounts). Sunset cruises depart between 4:00 P.M. and 6:30 P.M. depending on the time of year and the type of cruise you select.

> *"Until you are ready to look foolish, you'll never have the possibility of being great."*
>
> —CHER

Where to Find Sports, Recreation, and Outdoor Activities ◆ 107

Dance/Yoga

Coffeemill Dance & Yoga Studio

916 Pohalski Lane (305) 296-9982
www.coffeemilldance.com

With classes available seven days a week, you can find something to suit your style. Visit the website for times and prices.

Paradise Health & Fitness

1706 N. Roosevelt Avenue (305) 872-2675 or (305) 296-6348
www.paradisehealthandfitness.com

Explore all types of dance and exercise including ballroom, salsa, Pilates, pole dancing, yoga, step and stretch, and tone. Paradise is an island favorite, providing a casual and intimate atmosphere for you to relieve stress and get fit while having fun. Check the website for prices and class schedule.

Diving/Snorkeling

Sebago Catamarans

(305) 292-4768
www.keywestsebago.com

Sebago features a morning, afternoon, and combination snorkel, as well as instruction, sanitized snorkel gear, freshwater shower, free soft drinks, beer and wine, and easy access to the water via the sea ramp. The total excursion lasts 3 ½ hours, with morning and afternoon departures. Adult prices start at $49 per person. Visit the website for full details.

Subtropic Dive Centers

1605 N. Roosevelt Blvd.; (305) 296-9914
www.subtropic.com

Explore the water world with a dive trip. The centers feature morning, afternoon, and multi-day trips as well as instruction. Visit the website for times, prices, and more details.

Golf

Key West Golf Club

6450 College Rd.; (305) 731-6446
www.keywestgolf.com

A Rees Jones designed course, the club is a resort course that is open to the public and features Calloway club rentals. The unique Key West Golf Club's 18 holes encompass more than 200 acres of beautiful Florida Keys foliage and wildlife.

Movies

Tropic Cinema

416 Eaton St.; (305) 295-9493
http://www.keywestfilm.org/main.html

A popular place for new independent and foreign films as well as documentaries, Tropic Cinema offers a unique Key West movie experience. Adult tickets are $7. Visit the website for a complete schedule of showings.

Where to Find Sports, Recreation, and Outdoor Activities ◆ 109

Parasailing

Sunset Watersports

Four Key West locations; (305) 296-2554
www.sunsetwatersports.info

Experience the thrill and adventure of floating peacefully high above Key West. Fly alone or with a friend. Bring your camera for the breathtaking views of the tropical paradise. Call for prices and times.

Backcountry Adventures

Danger Charters

407 Caroline St. #A; (305) 296-3272
www.dangercharters.com

Featuring sailing, kayaking, and snorkeling, Danger provides island and back country adventures aboard the *Danger* and *Danger Cay* in the shallows of the Key West National Wildlife Refuge. Ask about their fabulous Wind & Wine. Prices vary based on excursion.

110 ◆ *Girls Getaway Guide to Key West*

Skydiving

Skydive Florida Keys

Sugarloaf Airport, 12 miles north of Key West; (305) 395-0555
SkydiveFloridaKeys.com

Enjoy an incomparable view of the Florida Keys and the crystal-clear waters around them while skydiving. Tandem jump prices start at $229. Videos and pictures are available to make sure you can show your family and friends just how adventurous you were during your vacation. Tours are offered daily from 10:00 A.M. until sunset from Sugarloaf Airport located at Mile Marker 17.

Theater

The Red Barn Theatre

319 Duval St., rear; (305) 296-9911
www.redbarntheatre.org

For more than a quarter-century the intimate Red Barn has been entertaining theatre fans in Key West with its live productions, including comedy, drama, cabaret shows, and musicals. Enjoy cocktails under the Royal Poinciana Trees in Zabar's Courtyard at the full-service bar before the curtain opens and during intermission. Show times are at 8:00 P.M., unless otherwise noted. Visit the website for a listing of upcoming shows.

Where to Find Sports, Recreation, and Outdoor Activities ◆ 111

Tennessee Williams Theater

5901 College Rd.; (305) 295-7676
www.twstages.com

With featured guests such as Joel Grey and shows like "The Great American Trailer Park Musical," this theater provides fantastic show opportunities. Presenters include: Key West Symphony Orchestra, Key West Pops Orchestra, Island Opera Theater, Paradise Big Band, and Keys Chorale. Ticket prices vary based upon show and seating. Call between 10:00 A.M.–4:00 P.M. for more details.

Waterfront Playhouse

Mallory Square in Old Historic Key West; (305) 294-5015
www.waterfrontplayhouse.com

As Florida's longest continuously running theatre company, the Key West Players strive to enhance a history of presenting dynamic, entertaining, and challenging live theatre for our diverse community of locals and tourists. Housed in the historic Waterfront Playhouse, the Key West Players have adopted Key West's official motto of "One Human Family," believing that theatre has a special power to reflect and illuminate the human experience. Visit the company's website for upcoming shows. Previous performances have included *Tuesdays with Morrie* and *Naked Boys*. Tickets are $30 and $35.

112 ◆ *Girls Getaway Guide to Key West*

Tours

Conch Train Tour

501 Front St.; (305) 294-5161
www.conchtourtrain.com

Since 1958, the Conch Train has been providing tours through Key West. The 90-minute tour begins at the Front Street Depot and ends in Mallory Square. The train will make one loop through Old Town Key West. There are two short stops, one at Station Depot and one at Flagler Station, which is where those who wish to can disembark to see the sights and choose to catch a later train. The narrated tour is led by your driver and tour guide. Adult price is $29; visit the website for discounts.

Ghost Tours of Key West

423 Fleming St.; (305) 294-9255
www.hauntedtours.com

This 90-minute, one-half mile tour departs each night from the Crowne Plaza—La Concha Hotel at 8:00 P.M. and 9:00 P.M. During the tour, which is led by a guide and lit by a lantern, you'll hear crazy and spooky tales of Key West residents and visitors. The tour, which has been in operation since 1996, has appeared on *Weird Travels* and *America's Most Haunted Places*. It is a fun way to learn more about Key West and to see interesting sights. Reservations are recommended. Adult prices are $18.

Where to Find Sports, Recreation, and Outdoor Activities ◆ 113

Old Town Trolley Tours of Key West

Mallory Square; (305) 296-6688
www.trolleytours.com

For more than 25 years, Old Town Trolleys has been showing visitors the best of Key West. The trolley has ten stops in various island locations, so you can get on and off as much as you want. My tour guide/driver recommended a walk through the cemetery, which features educational and unique tombstones, such as a deer tombstone and that of Bertha Roberts. With ten stops, you are sure to find the trolley everywhere. Visit the website for a complete list of stops and discounts. Adult tickets are $29.

Seaplanes of Key West

Key West International Airport
3471 S. Roosevelt Blvd.; (305) 294-0709
www.seaplanesofkeywest.com

Seaplanes of Key West fly 70 miles west of Key West, over the emerald waters of the Gulf of Mexico, to the Dry Tortugas, known for its marine life, pirate legends, and sheer unspoiled beauty. Complimentary snorkel gear and coolers with soft drinks are available. Seaplanes offers morning, afternoon, or full-day trips. Call for more details.

114 ◆ *Girls Getaway Guide to Key West*

Wine Tasting

Key West Winery

103 Simonton St. (at Front St.); (305) 292-1717
www.keywestwinery.com

Home of the Key Lime, Mango, and other award-winning tropical wines, this winery offers free wine tastings daily. The winery also features a large selection of gourmet foods, key lime products, unique gift items, and Island Art. They offer free parking in the back of the building off Front Street. Open daily until 6:00 P.M.

> *"A friend can tell you things you don't want to tell yourself."*
>
> —FRANCES WARD WELLER

CHAPTER 9

Where to Go for Side Trips

Although Key West itself certainly has enough activities to keep you busy, there are several great side trips that may be of interest to you. With so much history and natural beauty in the Florida Keys, you don't have to go very far for some very interesting excursions. From dolphins to more islands, you cannot go wrong with a road (or boat or plane) trip from Key West.

Dolphin Research Center

MM 59 bayside; (305) 289-0003
58901 Overseas Highway
Grassy Key, FL 33050-6019
www.dolphins.org

A not-for-profit, the center researches dolphin behavior and provides a home to a group of Atlantic bottlenose dolphins as well as sea lions. There are exhibits, regularly scheduled lagoon-side walking tours, and special programs featuring Atlantic bottlenose dolphins. "Dolphin Encounter" lets you swim with and interact with the dolphins, see dolphin experts lead behavior

116 ◆ *Girls Getaway Guide to Key West*

sessions, and even paint with the dolphins. Some programs require a 30-day advance reservation.

Hours: 9:00 A.M.–4:30 P.M. daily, except certain holidays. General admission: Adults $19.50; Seniors 55 and over $16.50; visit the website for a discount coupon.

Dry Tortugas

www.nps.gov/drto

About 70 miles west of Key West and 37 miles west of the Marqueseas Keys lies a cluster of seven islands, composed of coral reefs and sand, called the Dry Tortugas. Along with the surrounding shoals and waters, they make up Dry Tortugas National Park. The islands were discovered in 1513 by Spanish explorer Juan Ponce de León. The area is known for its famous bird and marine life, its legends of pirates and sunken gold, and its military past. Hours: The park is open all year. Admission: The entrance fee for the park is $5.00 for visitors 17 and older. The pass is valid for seven days. To get there, you'll have to take a ferry or plane. Visit www.yankeefleet.com or www.seaplanesofkeywest.com for more information on transportation.

> *"The happiest business in the world is that of making friends."*
>
> —ANNE THAXTER EATON

Where to Go for Side Trips ◆ 117

Little Palm Island

28500 Overseas Highway; (800) GET-LOST
Little Torch Key, FL 33042
www.littlepalmisland.com

The resort, which is 22 miles north of Key West, is an internationally acclaimed private island paradise, listed among the top resorts in the world by *Condé Nast Traveler* and *Travel+Leisure* magazine. It is just offshore of Little Torch Key and accessible only by boat or seaplane. With a lagoon-style pool, oversized hammocks, meditative Zen Garden, and cozy Great Room library, the resort encourages a world of serenity, including the SpaTerre. Children under 16 years of age and pets are not permitted on the island. The Little Palm Motor Yacht departs the Welcome Station every hour on the bottom of the hour from 7:30 A.M. until 9:30 P.M. Visit the website for special offers.

Pigeon Key

MM 47 Oceanside; (305) 289-0025
www.pigeonkey.org

This island was the original campsite for the workers who built the Overseas Railway and Seven Mile Bridge, which was described as the eighth wonder of the world when it was completed in 1912. A marine research foundation is housed in the old buildings. To get to the island, you can walk or take a ferry. Hours: 9:00 A.M.–5:00 P.M. daily.

CHAPTER 10

Annual Area Happenings

Key West is known for its fabulous annual happenings and events. It seems there is always something going on in this fun-loving city. This chapter presents some highlights of annual happenings and events. From boat racing to garden tours to literary seminars to seafood festivals to antiques, Key West hosts events for everyone. Be sure to call or to visit websites for exact dates each year.

January

Acura Key West Regatta

www.premiereracing.com; (781) 639-9545

Founded by *Yachting* magazine in 1988, this annual event has evolved into a nine-race series of windward/leeward racing with nearly 300 boats in 18 to 20 classes within four divisions. This event draws serious and party-loving sailing enthusiasts to Key West each January.

Annual Florida Keys Seafood Festival

(305) 292-4501

The Florida Keys Commercial Fisherman Association co-hosts this yearly seafood festival featuring live music and fresh seafood harvested and prepared by local fishermen. Free admission 11:00 A.M.–9:00 P.M. Bayview Park, corner of Truman and Eisenhower Avenues.

Key West Craft Show

(305) 294-0431

This annual event draws about one hundred regional and national artisans to Key West's Whitehead Street to display their works of jewelry, ceramics, and much more. Free admission between 10:00 A.M.–5:00 P.M. at the corner of Whitehead and Greene Streets.

Key West House and Garden Tour

www.oirf.org; (305) 294-9501

From January to March the Old Island Restoration Foundation presents five houses and garden tours. Fee is $25; times are 10:00 A.M.–4:00 P.M.

Key West Literary Seminar

www.keywestliteraryseminar.org; (888) 293-9291

Featuring workshops, panel discussions, and receptions with nationally and internationally respected writers.

February

Annual Key West Antiques Show

www.kwahs.com; (305) 296-3913

That's right, even Key West plays host to the antiques game, so be sure to bring your best appraiser's eye and any goods you'd like appraised to Fort East Martello.

Annual Pigeon Key Arts Festival

www.pigeonkey.net; (305) 743-7869

Nestled beneath the old Seven Mile Bridge, Pigeon Key once served as a construction and maintenance outpost for the Overseas Railway. This quaint island hosts the annual arts festival, drawing Marathon artists, food, and entertainment tucked in amongst the restored cottages of the historic island. Pigeon Key is approximately 40 miles north of Key West.

International Women's Flag Football Championship

www.iwffa.com; (888) GO-IWFFA

Top Gun babe Kelly McGillis occasionally serves as Grand Marshall at this international event featuring flag football teams from Europe, Central and South America, and Canada.

Old Island Days Art Festival

(305) 294-1241

The annual fine arts show is held each February on lower Whitehead Street in historic Old Town.

March

Annual Conch Shell Blowing Contest

www.oirf.org/events/conchshell.htm; (305) 294-9501

An Old Island Days tradition, this unique contest features novel sounds produced by contestants in several age categories as they attempt to make "music" on fluted conch shells at Ocean Key Resort & Spa.

Annual Key West Gardens Tour

(305) 294-3210

Every March, the Key West Garden Club guides horticulture lovers through five private Key West gardens. View tropical flora that have drifted to Key West throughout the years and its contribution to the island's rare beauty.

The Smart Ride: Miami to Key West

www.thesmartride.org; (866) 696-7701

In an effort to demonstrate support for those infected or affected by AIDS, The Smart Ride is a two-day, 165-mile bicycle ride from Miami to Key West. Riders help raise funds.

April

Annual Robert Frost Poetry Festival

(305) 296-3573

The festival features poetry and haiku workshops and readings and a poetry and haiku contest. Events are staged at the Robert Frost Cottage at the Heritage House Museum, where Frost spent many island winters.

Annual Taste of Key West

(305) 296-6196

Many area restaurants present tasty samples of their cuisine to benefit AIDS Help Inc. The culinary celebration takes place at the Truman Waterfront overlooking Key West Harbor.

Conch Republic Independence Celebration

(305) 294-2298

Parades, bed races, parties, and a wacky "drag race" commemorate the founding of the Conch Republic on April 23, 1982, in response to a U.S. Border Patrol roadblock that halted traffic in and out of the Florida Keys.

May

Key West Songwriters' Festival

www.kwswf.com; (305) 296-4222

The annual showcase of musical magic features Nashville's top performing songwriters, with concerts staged in intimate, audience-friendly island settings. The festival is presented by Hog's Breath Saloon.

July

Hemingway Days

www.hemingwaydays.net; (305) 296-2388 (look-alike); 294-0320 (literary)

The annual celebration of the legendary author's work and lifestyle features literary readings, a theatrical premiere, a short story competition, a fishing tournament, and a Sloppy Joe's look-alike contest.

August

Key West Lobsterfest

www.keywestlobsterfest.com; (305) 849-2706

In celebration of the sweet, juicy taste of the Florida lobster, Key West celebrates with Lobsterfest. Begin with the Lobsterfest Duval Crawl on Friday, then hit the street fair and live concert on Saturday. Finally, indulge in Sunday's lobster brunch.

October

Fantasy Fest

www.fantasyfest.net; (305) 296-1817

Likened to Mardi Gras, Fantasy Fest is an outrageous 10-day annual celebration with an active schedule of costume competitions, promenades and street fairs, and a grand parade featuring marching groups and lavish floats. Beware: many costumes consist only of paint.

Goombay Festival

www.goombay-keywest.org; (305) 797-7225

Held in Key West's historic Bahama Village neighborhood, the lively Goombay is known for its island-style food, handmade African arts and crafts, nonstop live entertainment, and dancing in the streets.

> *"Age is a question of mind over matter. If you don't mind, it doesn't matter."*
>
> —LEROY (SATCHEL) PAIGE

November

Key West Offshore Powerboat World Championship

www.superboat.com; (305) 296-6166

For thrill-seeking girls, this nautical extravaganza brings sleek boats racing over the seas at speeds of up to 100 mph to Key West. The championship event draws world-class racers and large

126 ◆ *Girls Getaway Guide to Key West*

crowds each year. Parades and cocktail parties with the racers punctuate the event. There is usually a charge wherever you decide to watch the race, so have cash available.

Parrot Heads in Paradise

www.phip.com

Fans of musician Jimmy Buffett flock to the island dubbed Margaritaville for their annual "Meeting of the Minds" convention.

December

Annual Key West Island Kwanzaa

(305) 294-0884 or (305) 295-8310

The Bahama Conch Community Land Trust honors ancestors of the African diaspora with ceremonies, rituals, and feasts. The event takes place from Christmas through January.

Key West New Year's Eve Celebrations

(305) 296-2388; (305) 293-9800; (305) 292-3302

The festivities include a "conch shell drop" at Sloppy Joe's Bar, 201 Duval St.; the descent of a six-foot red high heel shoe carrying drag queen Sushi at the Bourbon Street Pub/New Orleans House complex, 724 Duval St.; and the descent of a pirate wench from the mast of the tall ship *Liberty Clipper* in the island city's Historic Seaport.

CHAPTER 11

Personal Faves

I always get asked about my personal faves in Key West, so this chapter is dedicated to answering those questions. If your time in Key West is limited or you aren't sure where to begin, browse through this quick list to see what may interest you. Here are my faves at the time of publication (of course, they are subject to change):

Favorite Resort (tie): Casa Marina Resort & Beach Club *and* Ocean Key Resort & Spa

Favorite Bed & Breakfast: Simonton Court

Favorite Hotel: La Concha Crown Plaza

Favorite Tour: Conch Train

Favorite Clothing Store: Fast Buck Freddie's

Favorite Novelty Store: Peppers of Key West

Favorite Gallery: Luis Sottil Gallery

Favorite Tourist Attraction: Ernest Hemingway Home & Museum

Favorite Museum: Key West Museum of Art & History

Favorite Breakfast: Camille's

Favorite Lunch: Conch Republic Seafood Company

Favorite Dinner: Café Sole

Favorite Place Unique to Key West: Blue Heaven

Favorite Drink: Rum Runner

Favorite Spa: Caribbean Spa

Favorite Martini Spot: Virgilio's

Favorite Bar: Irish Kevin's and Rick's

Favorite Local Celeb: Captain Tony

Favorite Beach: Fort Zachary Taylor

Favorite Place to Watch Sunset: Mallory Square, Top of La Concha

Favorite Key Lime Pie: Kermit's Key West

Favorite Annual Event: Fantasy Fest

Favorite Recreational Activity: Snorkeling

Favorite Sunset Cruise: Danger's Wind & Wine

Favorite Side Trip: Little Palm Island

Favorite Hangout: Key West Art Bar

> *For new and exciting hotspots plus more faves,*
> *visit www.GirlsGetawayGuide.net.*

CHAPTER 12

Helpful Sources to Plan Your Trip

Key West is accustomed to hosting tourists, so it is not surprising that the city and other businesses provide a vast array of information that is helpful to planning your trip. This chapter highlights helpful websites as well as tips and information for getting around town and to Key West.

Greater Key West Chamber of Commerce

402 Wall St., Key West, FL 33040
(800) LAST-KEY
www.keywestchamber.org

Key West Business Guild

Supporting gay and lesbian travel since 1978
www.gaykeywestfl.com

> *"Life may not be the party we hoped for, but while we're here we should dance."*
>
> —UNKNOWN

Key West's Finest

1107 Key Plaza, Box #310, Key West, FL 33040
www.keywestfinest.com

Florida Keys & Key West Tourist Development Council
  (800) FLA-KEYS
  www.fla-keys.com

Newspapers

Key West Citizen, www.keysnews.com

www.Keynoter.com

Magazines

Key West Magazine, www.kwmag.com
Travelhost of Key West, www.travelhost.com

Radio

Radio Free Key West—www.myspace.com/radiofreekeywest—Plays Key West artists and Key West-related themes; heavily steeped in Americana.

WAIL 99.5 FM—Classic Rock
WCNK 98.7 FM—Country
WEOW 92.7 FM—Top 40
WIIS 107.1 FM—Adult Contemporary
WKEY 93.5 FM—Light Adult Contemprary
WPIK 102.5 FM—Spanish
WWUS 104.1 FM—Classic Hits

Helpful Sources to Plan Your Trip ◆ 131

Getting Around

Airports

Key West International Airport

www.keywestinternationalairport.com
(305) 296-5439
3491 S. Roosevelt Blvd.
Key West, FL 33040

Miami International Airport

www.miami-airport.com
(305) 876-7000

Boat Ferry

Key West Express

www.seakeywestexpress.com
(888) 539-2628

Offering boat ferry service to and from Key West from Ft. Myers, Miami, and Marco Island, Key West Express saves you from the headaches of driving. You'll enjoy the ride in the high-speed jet-drive vessel with air-conditioned and heated cabins. Visit the website for rates and schedules.

132 ◆ *Girls Getaway Guide to Key West*

Car Rental

Almost all the major car rental companies have offices in Key West. Be sure to visit their websites for more information. Please keep in mind, however, that parking is very limited in Key West. You'll notice that scooters and bicycles are a common form of transportation.

Mopeds/Scooters/Electric Cars/Bicycles

Crowne Plaza (La Concha Hotel)

430 Duval St., Key West, FL 33040
(305) 293-1112

Moped Hospital

(866) 296-1625
www.mopedhospital.com

The oldest moped rental company in Key West, it is located two blocks from the Old Town Duval Street area.

Paradise Scooter Rentals—two locations

www.paradisescooterrentals.com
112 Fitzpatrick St. (across from Kino's Sandal Factory)
(305) 292-6441

Second location:
Crowne Plaza—La Concha Hotel
430 Duval St.
(305) 293-1112

Helpful Sources to Plan Your Trip ◆ 133

Tropical Bicycle & Scooter Rentals

(305) 294-8136
www.tropicalrentacar.com
1300 Duval St., Key West, FL 33040

Serving Key West since 1982. Open daily 8:30 A.M.–5:30 P.M.

Pedicabs

Perfect Pedicab

401 Southard
(305) 292-0077
www.perfectpedicab.com

Since 1989, Perfect Pedicab has been moving people throughout Key West. Visit the website or call for tour information or a quick lift.

Taxis

Friendly Cab Co. (305) 295-5555
Five Sixes Cab: (305) 296-6666

Taxis are readily available at the airport to take you to your hotel after you fly in. For in-town cab rides, fares are on the meter, regardless of the number of passengers up to four. For four or more, a group rate of $4.50 per person is allowed. Key West is very small and well regulated. During special occasions, such as Fantasy Fest, the city designates cabs to charge a per person fee, currently $4.50 for groups.

If you plan to take a taxi out of town, negotiate your fare before you begin; there are no set regulations once you leave.

134 ◆ *Girls Getaway Guide to Key West*

Most cabs will charge no more than $2 per mile. For a trip around town, call one of the local cab services to arrange service or wave a cab down on the street.

There are also eight independent taxis in Key West, each with a phone number on its side. Hint: Most drivers will offer 20 percent off your return trip to the airport if you call the number on their business card.

Trolleys/Trains

Both the Old Town Trolley and the Conch Train are great ways to see Key West, travel to the sights, and gain interesting facts about this unique town.

Old Town Trolley

www.trolleytours.com
201 Front St., Key West, FL 33040
(800) 868-7482

Conch Train

201 Front St., Key West, FL 33040
www.conchtourtrain.com
(800) 868-7482

INDEX

7 Artists Gallery, 34, 74
801 Bourbon Bar and Cabaret, 96

A&B Lobster House, 48
Abaco Gold, 34
accommodations, 19–31
Acura Key West Regatta, 119
Afterdeck Bar and Louie's Backyard, 96
AIDS, 122
AIDS Help Inc., 123
Alan S. Maltz Gallery, 74
Alonzo's Oyster Bar, 48
Alpert, Kellie, 82
American Apparel, 34
Angelina's Pizza, 48
annual area happenings, 119–26
Annual Conch Shell Blowing Contest, 122
Annual Florida Keys Seafood Festival, 120
Annual Key West Antiques Show, 121
Annual Key West Gardens Tour, 122
Annual Key West Kwanzaa, 126
Annual Pigeon Key Arts Festival, 121
Annual Robert Frost Poetry Festival, 123

Annual Taste of Key West, 123
Archeo Gallery, 75
Arvid, Thomas, 75
Atocha, 91
Audubon House & Tropical Gardens, 88
Audubon, John James, 88
Aubuchon, Carl E., 22
Avalon Bed & Breakfast, 20
Aveda's Salon on Duval, 69

backcountry adventures, 109
Bad Ass Coffee House, 49
Bagatelle Restaurant, 49
Bahama Village, 16, 125
Banana Café, 49
Banyan Resort, 20–21
Bayview Park, 120
beaches, 17, 103–4
Beach House Swimwear, 35
Beads of Distinction, 35
Berry, Michael, 82
Besame Mucho, 35
birds, 10
Birdsey, Sandford, 85
Biton, 36
Black, Christine, 77

136 ◆ *Girls Getaway Guide to Key West*

Blais, René, 84
Blond Giraffe, 50
Blue, 36
Blue Cat, The, 36
Blue Heaven, 16, 50–51, 128
boating, 104
B.O.'s Fish Wagon, 51
Bourbon Street Pub, 126
A Boy and His Dog, 75
Budget Key West, 21
Buffett, Jimmy, 62, 96, 126
Busam, Martin, 63

Café, The, 51
Café Marquesa, 52
Café Sole, 52, 128
Calleja, Elizabeth, 77
Camille's Restaurant, 53–54, 128
Captain Tony, 96, 128
Captain Tony's Saloon, 96
Caribbean Spa, 70, 128
Caroline's, 53
car rentals, 132
Casa Marina Resort & Beach Club,
     21–22, 127
Casa, 325, 22
casual dress, 14
Charest-Weinberg Gallery, 76
Cheeseburger Key West, 54
Chef Correa, 53
chickens, 10
Childs, Janis, 77
Cocktail Party, 36
Coffeemill Dance & Yoga Studio, 107
Commodore Waterfront, 54
Commotion, 37
"Conch," 9

Conch Republic Independence
     Celebration, 123
Conch Republic Seafood Company,
     55, 128
Conch Shop, 55
Conch Train Tour, 112, 127, 134
Congress Jewelers, 37
Cowboy Bill's Honky Tonk, 97
Croce, Pat, 92
Croissants de France, 56
Crowne Plaza Key West—La Concha,
     22–23, 112, 132
Cuba! Cuba!, 37
Custom House, 90

Damn Good Food To-Go, 56
dance, 107
Danger Charters, 109, 128
Dewey House, 26–27
Discovery, 105
Discovery Undersea Tours Key West,
     105
diving, 107–8
Dolphin Research Center, 115–16
DoubleTree Grand Key Resort, 23–24
drag queens, 60, 95, 96, 100, 126
Dreaming Goddess Botique, 38
Dry Tortugas, 105, 113, 116
Dry Tortugas National Park, 116
Duval Crawl, 15, 124
Duval Gardens Bed & Breakfast, 24
Duval Street, 15, 21–24, 26, 28, 29,
     31, 34, 36, 39, 48, 49, 53, 54, 62–
     64, 67, 78, 83, 86, 95, 126

East Martello Museum and Gallery,
     76

Index ◆ 137

Egg, 77
Ego, 38
El Siboney Restaurant, 57
Emeralds International, Inc., 38
Ernest Hemingway Home &
    Museum, 88, 127
Evan & Elle, 39

Fantasy Fest, 125, 128, 133
Fast Buck Freddie's, 39, 127
Fat Tuesday, 97
Ferry, Susan, 52
Finnegan's Wake, 57
Fischer, Lynne, 77
Fisher, Mel, 91
Five Sixes Cab, 133
Flohr, Michael, 75
Florida Keys & Key West Tourist
    Development Council, 130
Florida Keys Commercial Fisherman
    Association, 120
Florida Keys Eco-Discovery Center,
    93
Fogarty's Bar & Restaurant, 58
Fort Zachary Taylor Beach, 17, 20,
    103–4, 128
Fort Zachary Taylor State Park, 20,
    103–4
Fresh Produce, 40
Friendly Cab Co., 133
Front Street Depot, 112
Frost, Robert, 73, 89
Fury Water Adventures, 106

galleries, 73–87
Gallery Key West, 77
Gallery on Greene, 77

Garden of Eden, 97
Gardens Hotel, 24–25, 80
getting around, 131–34
Ghost Tours of Key West, 112
Gingerbread Square Gallery, 77
glass bottom boats, 105
Glass Renunions, 78
Godard, Michael, 84
golf, 108
Goombay Festival, 125
Grand Key Resort Beach Club, 23
Grand Vin, 98
Greater Key West Chamber of
    Commerce, 129
Green Parrot Bar, 98
Grey, Joel, 111
Guild Hall, 78

Haitian Art Company, 79
Hands On, 79
Harborwalk, 31, 56
Hard Rock Café, 58
Harpoon Harry's, 58–59
Harrison, Ben, 80
Harrison Gallery, 80
Harrison, Helen, 80
Harry S. Truman Little White House,
    89
Helio Gardens Gallery, 80
Hemingway Days, 124
Hemingway, Ernest, 16, 23, 41, 45,
    73, 88, 90, 96, 100, 124
Hemingway Look-a-Like Contest,
    100, 124
Heyman, Richard, 77
Higgs Beach, 17
Historic Seaport, 16–17, 56, 59

138 ◆ *Girls Getaway Guide to Key West*

Hobbs, Pam, 77
Hog's Breath Saloon, 98–99, 124
Hot Tin Roof, 59
hurricane season, 12, 14

International Women's Flag Football
    Championship, 121
Irish Kevin's, 99
Isaac Allerton, 91
Island Arts Co-op, 81
Island City House Hotel, 25
Island Dogs Bar, 99
Island Opera Theater, 111
Islescapes Dinner Cruise, 59

Johnson, J. Seward, 90
Jones, Rees, 108
Joy Gallery, 81

kayaking, 106
Kelly's Caribbean Bar, Grill &
    Brewery, 60
Kennedy Gallery, 81
Kennedy, Robert, 81
Kent Gallery, 82
Kermit's Key West Key Lime Shoppe,
    40, 128
Key Accents Home & Garden, 41
key lime pie, 40, 50, 54, 128
Key Lime Pie Festival, 50
Keys Chorale, 111
Key West Aloe, 41
Key West Aquarium, 93
Key West Art and Historical Society, 90
Key West Bed & Breakfast, The
    Popular House, 26
Key West Bight, *see* Historic Seaport

Key West Business Guild, 129
Key West Butterfly & Nature
    Conservatory, 20, 86, 94
Key West Citizen, 130
Key West Craft Show, 120
Key West Express Ferry, 12, 14, 131
Key West Gallery, 82
Key West Golf Club, 108
Key West Golf Course, 24
Key West Harbor, 123
Key West Heritage House Museum &
    Robert Frost Cottage, 89, 123
Key West House and Garden Tour,
    120
Key West International Airport, 12,
    23, 131
Key West Island Books, 41
Key West Kayaking, 106
Key West Literary Seminar, 120
Key West Lobsterfest, 124
Key West Magazine, 130
Key West Museum of Art & History,
    90, 128
Key West New Year's Eve Celebra-
    tions, 126
Key West Players, 111
Key West Pops Orchestra, 111
Key West Offshore Powerboat World
    Championship, 125–26
Key West's Finest, 129
Key West Ship Channel, 104
Key West Shipwreck Historeum
    Museum, 90–91
Key West Songwriters' Festival, 99, 124
Key West Symphony Orchestra, 111
Key West Winery, 114
Kinkade, Thomas, 86

Index ◆ 139

Kino Sandals, 42
Kiraly, John, 77
Klein, Calvin, 20
Klein, David, 85
Koziol, Tippi, 87
Kravitz, Boris, 79
Kravitz, Ruth, 79
Kush, Christopher, 45
KWest, 99
KW Light Gallery, 83

La Concha Hotel, 100, 127, 128
La Mer Hotel, 26–27
La Te Da, 60, 100
Latitudes, 61
La Trattoria Venezia, 61
Liberty Clipper, 126
Lighthouse & Keepers Quarters
     Museum, 91
Lilly Pulitzer, 42
Little Palm Island, 117, 128
Little Torch Key, 117
Local Color, 42
Louie's Backyard, 62
Lucky Street Gallery, 83
Luis Sottil Gallery, 83, 127

Mack, Bill, 83
MacNelly, Jeff, 77
Mallory Square, 7, 14, 15, 20, 49,
     112, 128
Maltz, Alan S., 74
Mangoes, 62
Margaritaville, 126
Marti, José, 60
Martin's Café Restaurant, 63
Mary O'Shea's Glass Garden, 84

McCall, Bernadette, 85
McCall, John, 85
McConnell, Sean, 98
McDonough, Irene, 97
McGillis, Kelly, 60, 121
McHugh, C.B., 44
Mel Fisher Maritime Heritage Society
     & Museum, 91
Miami International Airport, 12, 131
Miano, Kate, 24
Michaels, 63
Miller, David, 75
Moped Hospital, 132
movies, 108
museums, 73, 88–92

National Register of Historic Places,
     21, 26, 62
nature attractions, 73, 93–94
New Orleans House, 126
nightlife, 95–101
Nine One Five, 64

Ocean Key Resort & Spa, 27, 59, 122,
     127
Oh My Godard Gallery, 84
Old Island Days, 122
Old Island Days Arts Festival, 121
Old Town, 7, 16, 24, 25, 29, 30, 66,
     69, 112, 121
Old Town Trolley Tours of Key West,
     113, 134
Overseas Railway, 117

Paint Key West, 85
Palmer, Michael, 77
Pan American Airlines, 60

140 ◆ *Girls Getaway Guide to Key West*

Papio, Stanley, 76
Paradise Big Band, 111
Paradise Health & Fitness, 107
Paradise Scooter Rentals, 132
parasailing, 109
parking, 14
Parrot Heads in Paradise, 126
Pat Croce's Pirate Soul Museum, 92
Peachey, Kate, 85
Pepe's Café, 64
Peppers of Key West, 43, 127
Perfect Pedicab, 133
personal faves, 127–28
Pier House Resort & Caribbean Spa, 28
Pigeon Key, 117
Pisces, 65
planning your trip, 129–30
Ponce de León, Juan, 116
Porter, Jessie, 89
Prana Spa, 70

radio stations, 130
Ray, Rachael, 51
Reach Resort, 28
Red Barn Theater, 110
Red Door Gallery, 84
restaurants, 47–67
Restaurant Store, 43
Ripley's Believe It or Not! Key West, 92
Robert Frost Poetry Festival, 89
Roberts, Bertha, 113
Robert the Doll, 76

Salem, Jim, 77
Sanchez, Mario, 77
Santa Margarita, 91

Seaplanes of Key West, 113
Sebago Catamarans, 107
Senses at Play Exotic Fine Art Gallery, 85
Seven Mile Bridge, 117
Shades of Key West, 43
shopping, 33–45
side trips, 115–17
Sign of Sandford, 85
Simon, 75
Simonton Court Historic Inn & Cottages, 29, 127
Skydive Florida Keys, 110
skydiving, 110
Sky, Jasmine, 38
Sloppy Joe's Bar, 96, 100, 124, 126
Smart Ride: Miami to Key West, 122
Smathers Beach, 17, 104
Smith, Wayne, 77
snorkeling, 107–8, 128
Solar Spa, 71
Sottil, Luis, 83
South Beach, 17
Southernmost Hotel on Duval Street, 29
Southernmost on the Beach, 29
Southernmost Point, 20
spas and salons, 69–71
SpaTerre—Ocean Key Resort & Spa, 71
Sponge Market, 44
sports, recreation, and outdoor activities, 103–17
Steininger, Ellen, 79
Stone Soup Gallery, 85
Strip House, 65
Subtropic Dive Centers, 108

Index ◆ 141

Sugar Apple, 44
Sugarloaf Airport, 110
Sunset Cigar Co., 44
sunset cruise, 106
Sunset Key, 30, 61
Sunset Key Guest Cottages, 30
Sunset Watersports, 109
Sushi, 96, 126
Suzy Starfish, 86
Symons, David, 36

Tabora, Roy Gonzalez, 82
taxis, 133–34
temperatures, 12
Tennessee Williams Theater, 111
theater, 110–11
Thomas Kinkade, 86
Top of La Concha, 100
tours, 112–13
Travelhost of Key West, 130
Tropical Bicycle & Scooter Rentals, 133
Tropic Cinema, 108
Truman, Harry S., 73, 89
Truman Waterfront, 123
Truval Village Market Place, 45
Turtle Kraals Restaurant & Bar, 66, 101
Two Friends Bar, 66

U.S. 1, 9, 14, 98

Van Aken, Norman, 52
Virgilio's, 101, 128
Voltaire Books Key West, 45

walking, 14
Warhol, Andy, 65
Waterfront Market, 84
Waterfront Playhouse, 111
Wells, Sharon, 83
Westin Key West Resort & Marina, 30, 31, 61
Wilkins, Dawn, 80
Williams, Tennessee, 23, 41, 45
Willie T's, 67
Wilson, Jessica, 77
wine tasting, 114
Wings of Imagination, 86
Wyland, 87
Wyland Galleries of Key West, 87

Yankee Freedom II, 105
yoga, 107

Zbyszek, 87
Zbyszek Gallery, 87
Zolotow, Dianne, 83

Give the Gift of
Girls Getaway Guide to Key West
Leave Your Baggage at Home
to Your Friends and Colleagues

CHECK YOUR LEADING BOOKSTORE OR ORDER HERE

❏ YES, I want _____ copies of *Girls Getaway Guide to Key West* at $13.95 each, plus $4.95 shipping per book (Florida residents please add 98¢ sales tax per book). Canadian orders must be accompanied by a postal money order in US funds. Allow 15 days for delivery.

My check or money order for $_____ is enclosed.

Please charge my: ❏ Visa ❏ MasterCard
 ❏ Discover ❏ American Express

Name _____

Organization _____

Address _____

City/State/Zip _____

Phone_____ Email _____

Card # _____

Exp. Date_____ Signature _____

Please make your check payable and return to:
Gray Dog Publishing
P.O. Box 2589, Orlando, FL 32802
For credit card orders, visit:
www.GirlsGetawayGuide.net